IDENTITY IS DESTINY

Identity Is Destiny

LEADERSHIP AND THE ROOTS OF

VALUE CREATION

LAURENCE D. ACKERMAN

Berrett-Koehler Publishers, Inc.
San Francisco

Berrett-Koehler Publishers, Inc.
450 Sansome Street, Suite 1200
San Francisco, CA 94111-3320
Tel: (415) 288-0260
Fax: (415)362-2512
www.bkconnection.com

Ordering Information
Quantity sales. Special discounts are available on quantity purchases by corporations, associations, and others. For details, contact the "Special Sales Department" at the Berrett-Koehler address above.

Individual sales. Berrett-Koehler publications are available through most bookstores. They can also be ordered direct from Berrett-Koehler: Tel: (800) 929-2929; Fax: (802) 864-7626; www.bkconnection.com.

Orders for college textbook/course adoption use.
Please contact Berrett-Koehler:
Tel: (800) 929-2929; Fax: (802) 864-7626.

Orders by U.S. trade bookstores and wholesalers. Please contact Publishers Group West, 1700 Fourth Street, Berkeley, CA 94710. Tel: (510) 528-1444; Fax (510) 528-3444.

Printed in the United States of America

Printed on acid-free and recycled paper that is composed of 50% recovered fiber, including 10% post consumer waste).

Library of Congress Cataloging-in-Publication Data

Ackerman, Laurence D., 1950–
    Identity is destiny : leadership and the roots of value creation /
        Laurence D. Ackerman.
        p. cm.
    Includes bibliographical references and index.
    ISBN 1-57675-068-X
    1. Corporate image. 2. Leadership. I. Title.
HD59.2 .A28 1999
658.4'092—dc21   99-05534

First Edition
05   04   03   02   01   00   10   9   8   7   6   5   4   3   2   1

Dedicated to my father, Jack, my son, Max, and Russ Anspach, mentor and friend.

CONTENTS

PREFACE

Since the term became popular some fifty years ago, *corporate identity* has been used largely in its narrowest, most superficial sense: names, logotypes, and advertising tag lines—all of them primary components of corporate marketing.

These high-profile "identity" elements are fabricated by well-intended professionals to reflect current business trends (such as globalization and technology). Sometimes they are designed to mimic the look and feel of *most admired* companies in hopes of gaining some positive rub-off. With rare exceptions, these manufactured identities are devoid of any traceable connection to the unique, value-creating characteristics that distinguish the company they are created to represent.

It is no wonder that many business managers have questioned the value of "corporate identity." It is also no surprise that so-called "identities" are discarded and created anew with seeming ease and little regret. In more cases than not, what we have come to refer to as corporate identity lacks the integrity that commands respect.

More recently, the notion of identity has begun to take on a deeper meaning. In a *Conference Board* survey report on post-merger integration, published in July 1999, three factors were cited as being instrumental in creating a framework for designing a successful new organization. At the top of the list was a company's *basic identity, core values, and business strategy.* Numbers two and three, respectively, were *the underlying economic model of the enterprise* and *the philosophy and style of the CEO.*

The *Conference Board* research goes on to describe how "the firm's identity, supported by its core values and business strategy, helps to create a common understanding and commitment among all employees." This is progress, but there is still a long way to go.

In the field of human behavior and psychology, the notion of identity reflects the things that make a person unique—the rich and varied set of traits that fuels differentiation and inspires contribution. Within this field, identity stands as the single most powerful force. In failing to apply this deeper definition of identity to "corporate beings" as well, we have done business a great disservice; indeed, we have perpetrated a fraud upon ourselves. Without intending to, organizations have violated the true meaning—and thus the value—of identity, leaving its productive potential untapped.

What we have done by not embracing identity in its fullest sense is to create an organizational vacuum that is taking a severe toll on leaders' ability to do their jobs—to help employees love their work and deliver results that mirror their passion, to get customers to want to do business with their companies as a "life priority," and to elicit from investors a commitment to stay with the company in the face of inevitable financial ups and downs.

Who are we? What do we stand for? How are we different? Where do I fit in? During the thousands of interviews I have conducted over the years, I have found that these are the questions that weigh most heavily on managers and employees. And it is to the CEO, or to the head of the division or business unit, that they invariably look for the answers.

Being able to answer these questions demands a keen knowledge of a company's identity—not its name, symbol, or slogan, but the true identity of the institution, which has deep roots and contains its own integrity.

There is only one way forward, and that is to recognize and respond to identity as a governing force in shaping the fortunes of each organization and of everyone whose lives it touches. My purpose in writing this book is to set this process in motion and, as a result, to change how—*and why*—leaders lead.

ACKNOWLEDGMENTS

One person above all others has made this book more readable, even richer, than it otherwise might have been: Gerry Sindell. Ever since I first met Gerry over the telephone in March 1996—he had "introduced himself" to me via a letter—he has taken a special interest in the story of identity-based management. He has become a champion of the Laws of Identity. He has made them his own.

The best way to describe Gerry's contribution to *Identity Is Destiny* is to invoke a decidedly old-fashioned, rarely used term: *midwife*. From conception through birth, this book has been a five-year effort, at times no less than an ordeal. Gerry has been there through it all, as my writing coach, my editor, my alter ego, my friend, and, when I needed it, even my conscience concerning whether what I was writing was really what I wanted to say.

In an early "think" session in my kitchen in the spring of 1996, Gerry and I were talking about how to structure this book. I had worked through and discarded three, maybe four, different approaches in the previous two years. I had started and abandoned at least that many drafts.

The subject at the moment was the uniqueness of organizations. I was describing to Gerry, rather passionately, what I had learned in my consulting experience—that every company is unique and that the individuality of each is the wellspring of differentiation. Gerry looked up and after a momentary pause asked me a question; he asked whether I wasn't in fact describing what amounted to a *natural law*. Then Gerry asked a larger question, the answer to which became the framework for this book: *In all of my descriptions about the impact of identity on people as well as organizations, was I suggesting that identity embodies natural laws that apply to both?*

Gerry Sindell helped me find my voice, and for that I will be forever grateful. His is a gift of insight that, leavened with empathy, patience, and creativity, has helped make this a better book and me a wiser person.

I owe another large debt of gratitude to Russ Anspach. In the years I worked with Russ at the firm he helped found, Anspach Grossman Portugal, he taught me to always *go further*—in the questions I asked, in my analyses of client situations, and, most important, in the *significance* of the conclusions I drew. Russ has a passion for truth that was addictive and inspiring. He helped me find that passion in myself and express it in the name of integrity.

Others too deserve special credit for their unerring belief in the subject of *Identity Is Destiny* and their willingness to be there when I needed them. My agent, Natasha Kern, "speaks" the language of identity. She is a champion of identity-based living and was relentless in marketing the proposal for *Identity Is Destiny* until a deal was done with the right publisher.

My wife, Janet, was a reviewer of ideas and words off and on during the time it has taken to create this book. As a seasoned finance professional with rigorous common sense and an eye for detail, she "tested" much of my thinking along the way. Jan helped me make sure that many of the practical implications of identity were clear on a case-by-case basis. My thanks to her also for being patient and supportive during the long stretches of time I disappeared behind my computer.

In this vein, I also want to thank my son, Max, who is now nearly eleven years old. During the five years that completing this project has taken, Max developed a genuine interest in "Dad's book." He came to ask routinely how it was going and whether I thought people would like it. His understanding and patience—specifically, his willingness to wait for me to finish a work session before we played ball—was a great "small gift" that I will always treasure.

I extend my final acknowledgment to the clients whose stories I tell in this book. To them I owe perhaps my greatest thanks. In all cases, the executives and employees of these fine organizations enabled me to learn the secrets of identity while I was helping them meet their own needs. In being part of this book, these companies, individually and collectively, are giving to all institutions a gift that is quite exceptional; they are helping to illuminate the path to value creation that is inherent in identity. They are, in a very real sense, the teachers of the Laws of Identity and the "heroes" of this work.

INTRODUCTION: LEADERSHIP MEETS IDENTITY

For all the study and writing on leadership, the subject still retains an air of mystery that fuels our curiosity and impels us to learn more. Leadership is the prerequisite of all other things: of change, of growth, of achievement.

When we think of leadership we typically think of individuals who demonstrate courage under fire, boldness in the face of uncertainty, determination against all odds. We often look upon those in leadership positions as larger-than-life figures, somehow different from the rest of us. In business we point to such people as Louis Gerstner at IBM, Percy Barnevik of Asea Brown Boveri, Andrea Jung of Avon, and Jack Welch at General Electric. On the world stage we single out the likes of Nelson Mandela, Franklin Delano Roosevelt, and Mahatma Ghandi. All of these individuals have demonstrated varying degrees of courage, boldness, and determination.

But if leadership demands anything, it first demands insight—into people, organizations, circumstances, and situations. Without the knowledge that comes with insight, all the courage in the world can amount to nothing—or worse. Misplaced, it can destroy fine organizations and wreak havoc with the lives of employees; it can even lead the world into war.

1

The advent of the information age—the age of the knowledge worker—has made leadership harder than ever. From the leader's perspective, command and control do not work very well anymore, because it is impossible to "command" people to think a certain way or to share knowledge they simply choose not to share. Intellectual capital is now as important as financial capital in business planning and execution. The trend toward ever-greater knowledge continues to slice through the historically more physical, unitized world of business described long ago by Frederick Taylor and Alfred Sloan. It is an unstoppable trend, turbo-boosted by the Internet, that is leading us to new ways of perceiving and solving problems and, in the process, altering our beliefs about what begets success.

Walls are coming down, though not without difficulty, between company divisions and between such traditionally self-contained functions as marketing, sales, R&D, manufacturing, engineering, finance, and communications. The "white spaces" between them all—divisions and functions alike—are fertile ground for identifying new business opportunity.

Walls are coming down in other ways as well. Traditional lines of demarcation between competitors are being crossed regularly through joint ventures and strategic alliances designed to boost productivity and expand markets. The result is an atmosphere in which it is not surprising to see Bill Gates bail out Steve Jobs, his long-time rival, by investing in Apple Computer.

Taken together, what do these changes mean? They herald the early stages of a period driven above all by the *mechanics of integration* rather than of unitization—the integration of experience, ideas, information, relationships, and, of course, the knowledge that is the net result of it all. The power of contemporary leaders will depend increasingly on their ability to perceive and act upon the whole, adopting a truly *integrated* view of life.

It is in the realm of integration that leadership and identity meet head on. Identity, as I have come to know it, is the unique characteristics of an organization, or individual, which are the *integrated result* of particular mental, physical, and emotional capacities. Consider it the "soft rock" that is the center of all things human. Leaders who have a firm understanding of identity can look at the world in an integrated way, blending external and internal experiences and events to produce a unified "story" about how things are—or how they might be. Perceiving the world through the lens of identity can provide leaders with perhaps the only reliable road map for navigating the turbulent future.

HISTORY SETS THE STAGE

Over time, I have watched as business organizations have moved slowly but relentlessly toward their inevitable encounter with their own identities. It is an evolution spurred by the mechanics of integration, which are evident in many of the trends that have defined management priorities and practices over the past two decades.

The march toward acknowledging identity gained momentum in the early 1980s, with the rise of corporate culture as an accepted business concept. The popular book *Corporate Cultures* sparked awareness of the vital role that beliefs and human behavior play in a company's success. One of the book's major contributions was demonstrating how culture "integrates" people across divisional and functional lines.

Around the same time, managers began to think seriously about vision and mission as part of the strategic lexicon of their companies. They discovered that well-crafted mission statements framed strategy in ways people could understand at all levels of business activity, from the executive suite to truck drivers, line workers, and customer service representatives. Apple Computer's original mission, to "humanize the computer," and Maytag's recent aim, to "own the home," are two good examples. Managers found that one of the most powerful features of a robust corporate mission was its ability to bring people together to achieve a common goal.

In the late 1980s and early 1990s, the notion of corporate competencies lent further credence to human characteristics—skills and expertise that integrated multiple disciplines—as the essence of effective strategy. Sustainable competitive advantage was born of these competencies, rather than from the company's technology, capital base, or products and services. The work of Gary Hamel and C. K.

Prahalad was instrumental in helping managers recognize the existence, and the relevance, of their organization's core competencies.

More recently, managers have paid serious attention to the idea that successful organizations are united by a purpose that transcends profit. Although such "purpose" yields economic rewards, it also acknowledges the primacy of the human institution in the value creation process. The leading exponents of corporate purpose have been James Collins and Jerry Porras, whose book *Built to Last* clarified the importance of purpose and other nonfinancial drivers behind what they describe as "visionary" companies.

Coincidental with the rise of corporate missions, competencies, and purpose, managers have focused increasingly on the corporate brand as a vital part of a company's selling proposition. The name *Gillette* adds inestimable value to the Sensor product line. IBM, American Express, and Intel are "maker's marks" that inspire consumers' confidence in the products they buy from these organizations. What is significant is that the "brand," in all of these cases, is informed as much by a corporation's culture and competencies as by the features and benefits of its products.

The mechanics of integration are most dramatically evident today in globalization, which, in its own unique way, is prodding companies to wrestle with the notion of identity more seriously than ever before. Globalization is forcing a slow but steady integration of national markets and economies. Within far-flung organizations, it is driving the integration of experience, talents, beliefs, and passions among people who don't know each other, who come from different countries, and who don't speak the same language or share the same customs. Yet these people have been brought together to compete in territories where there is no end to the challenges they are being asked to meet. "Who are we?" has never been a more pressing question.

From a historical perspective, one of the most influential thinkers about leadership and identity over the past four decades has been Dr. Abraham Zaleznik of Harvard University. In his classic 1963 *Harvard Business Review* article, "The Human Dilemmas of Leadership," Dr. Zaleznik wrote, "The exercise of leadership requires a strong sense of identity—knowing who one is and who one is not—a sense of autonomy, separateness, or identity permits a freedom of action and thinking that is necessary for leadership." Dr. Zaleznik's focus was on the individual. What I have come to see is that this same sense of identity exists equally for organizations. Its presence shakes to the very roots the notion of what leadership, and management generally, are all about.

In an article in *Forbes* magazine in October 1998, Peter Drucker asserts that management is a social discipline that deals with "the behavior of people and social institutions." He continues, "The social universe has no 'natural laws' as the physical sciences do. It is thus subject to continuous change. This means that assumptions that were valid yesterday can become invalid and, indeed, totally misleading in no time at all."

In this book I argue otherwise. There are, in fact, natural laws that are ever-present. These laws provide a framework around which assumptions can and must be made. Unlike the physical laws of nature that derive from the external world, however, these laws flow from within; they flow from identity, governing business life just as they govern life itself. How these laws work—how they influence every organization and individual—is the subject of *Identity Is Destiny*.

In the past two decades, I have worked with over thirty CEOs and their management teams, helping them come to terms with the identity of their organizations—who those organizations are, what they stand for, and what to do about it. What I have learned firsthand is as much about what leadership is not as about what it is. Leadership is not simply about the CEO, or about other members of top management, or even about outstanding middle or junior managers who are making their marks in far corners of the organization. It certainly is not defined by one's job, position, or title. Nor is leadership just about leading groups of people within organizations. Markets are led, industries are led, societies are led.

From this perspective, I believe that leadership is best understood as an entire way of life; a way of living that is a function of one's identity—the identity of the individual, or the identity of the organization. How identity plays out in the life of an individual, or in the life of an enterprise, is the true test of the leadership mettle of each.

Leaders come in many forms. Meaningful contributions that significantly affect the lives of others are made, for instance, by people whose work requires solitude: software designers and writers among them. To these professionals, add scientists, researchers, and others who, by virtue of their talent and discoveries, often wind up "leading" others. Daniel Yankelovich, innovator of psychographic market segmentation in the early 1960s and founder of Yankelovich Partners, is a prime example. So are Thomas Edison and Peter Drucker.

As a way of life, leadership means *find yourself, be yourself, show yourself.* Because people regard leaders as special, leadership has become a framework for coming to terms with one's special capacities—one's identity—and then living accordingly. Leadership is not centered on life at the top; it is centered simply on life. The moment we recognize this fact, we are in a position to see that leadership begins as that solitary step wherein we first assume responsibility for leading ourselves. Leadership with a big "L" transforms into leadership with a small "l," a more humbling act of self-accountability that, once undertaken, may or may not result in our leading others.

From this vantage point, authenticity precedes authority, which helps to explain why so many entrepreneurs—Ted Turner, Mary Kay Ash, Michael Dell, Konosuke Matsushita—are held up as examples of true leaders. Their success is a by-product of living according to their identity.

In light of a corporation's identity, the responsibility for leadership belongs to the entire organization; it is no longer the province of a select few. The first aim that goes along with this collective responsibility is to lead the market on the strength of the company's unique, value-creating potential. A second aim follows closely on the heels of market leadership; it is societal leadership—the ability of a company to bring about positive, permanent social change as a result of managing through its identity, and to make money doing so.

A few years ago, I had an opportunity to work with Ernst & Young when the firm was in the midst of reengineering its global audit practice. What came to light was that this seemingly undifferentiable organization (a popular view is that all Big Five firms are largely the same) had clear and distinctive characteristics all its own. What I saw was that E&Y's identity lay in its all-encompassing capacity to *create capital advantage* for clients. This capacity came to life in terms of financial advantage, operational advantage, and competitive advantage.

But E&Y's contribution in the marketplace transcended its relationship with clients. The institutional role of this enterprise—its contribution not only to its clients, but to society at large—was also inherent in its identity. "Creating capital advantage" was the key to unlocking E&Y's potential to provide greater security to investors and others who rely on the integrity of balance sheets and the economic soundness of corporations.

In spite of the millions of hours, and billions of dollars, dedicated to analyzing why things work or don't work, many companies are focusing on too narrow a set of factors. They study with great discipline vital forces such as production economics, market demand, customer preferences, organization design, culture, and business processes in order to improve the profit and loss statement and balance sheet. New analytical techniques, such as economic value-added (EVA), are developed and lend further credence to self-examination activities.

Often, however, the "mysteries" of success and failure remain veiled. For instance, why did Westinghouse die? Were economic or management weaknesses addressed too late? Was it because the company lacked visionary leadership? Why have so many companies, born decades ago, simply gone away? Did they become anachronisms by stubbornly selling products that people no longer needed or wanted?

Cutting through all the complexities of business and competition today, I believe that the essential reason why these companies disappeared is that managers didn't pay attention to the inherent identity of their organizations; they failed to take stock of the company's unique, value-creating characteristics.

In attempting to figure out why things happen, we as individuals and "we" as organizations—from senior executives and middle managers to rank-and-file employees—spend too much time attending to observable facts and change levers. By contrast, we spend too little time assessing who we are underneath it all—underneath the assumptions about ourselves as "parent" or "spouse," "manager" or "employee," or, in the case of organizations, underneath the strategies, divisions, functions, products and services, and even cultures that constitute the most easily discerned, commonly accepted parts of the enterprise.

I was twenty-five before I began to suspect that things don't "just happen," and it took me another twenty years to unravel the mystery of why they do. Thus I have been the subject of my own experiment and have studied my clients as well. All these experiences and observations have convinced me that there is a reason for how life unfolds and that knowing that reason is priceless.

By way of personal example, my decision to join Anspach Grossman Portugal rather than Arthur D. Little when I was thirty was a gut decision; it simply felt right. I knew that ADL would lend prestige to my career following a two-and-a-half-year stint with Yankelovich, Skelly & White. But I was viscerally drawn to AGP, then a relatively new and small player in the world of corporate identity consulting. I was drawn, as I now see, to the holistic concept of identity rather than to what I saw as the more traditional field of management consulting. I was equally drawn to the extraordinary impact that identity can have in unifying an organization. Looking back, it was a decision that was in perfect harmony with what I was later to learn were the Laws of Identity.

Five years earlier, I had taken a job with Filene's in Boston. It lasted six months. My joining Filene's was in direct conflict with the Laws of Identity. I had ignored—in truth, I wasn't yet aware of—the inviolate facts of life as prescribed by these laws. I didn't realize that my relationship with others (in this case, Filene's) would be only as strong as the natural alignment between my identity and the store's. As I learned, I had no aptitude for retailing and no genuine attraction to it. There could hardly have been two more disparate "beings."

As I have worked with business executives on a broad spectrum of identity challenges, I have also worked to understand and live according to my own identity. It has been a journey with many surprises—sobering discoveries about my past, exhilarating insights into my true strengths, and (maybe most important) a clear understanding of my potential for making a contribution in this world and being rewarded in return.

For my clients as for myself, there have been right decisions and wrong ones. In some of these cases, the correct turn should have been apparent as we approached the crossroads, others only by the rearview mirror. It has taken more than the past twenty years for me to understand fully the forces that have accounted for these turns.

What I finally came to see, only in the last few years, is that identity contains its own logic. Many of the most memorable events in my life could be explained in relation to *who I am and who I am not.* Events surrounding my clients could be understood in the same way, as dependent on who the company was and who it was not. Seeing the world this way has evolved into a life discipline that I now employ religiously. The insights it yields contain their own wisdom— stop signs and red flags, but also flashing opportunities waiting to be seized.

In the summer of 1996, my family and I spent a week at the Home Ranch in Clark, Colorado. It was there, sitting alone in the anteroom of our cabin, that I realized that the logic of identity actually flowed from a definable set of *laws* that clarified so much about what works and what doesn't work in life, whether for an individual or for a business organization made up of tens or even hundreds of thousands of individuals. What I understood at that moment was that people and organizations are governed equally by these Laws of Identity—natural laws that explain past events and foreshadow the future.

In discerning these laws, I also discovered that they exist in a certain pattern, a distinct sequence that amplifies their logic and imbues them with additional meaning. Taken in this sequence, the laws form a credo—the *identity credo*—that speaks to organizations as well as individuals. Both are ordered by identity as the inescapable center of gravity that organizes everything we are and do.

In the identity credo, "I" becomes as much the pronoun of the organization as that of the individual (*I*, Alcoa; *I*, Maytag). The eight laws of identity and the credo they reveal are as follows:

I. THE LAW OF BEING
Any organization composed of one or more human beings is alive in its own right, exhibiting distinct physical, mental, and emotional capacities that derive from, but transcend, the individuals who make up that organization over time.

"I am alive,"

II. THE LAW OF INDIVIDUALITY
An organization's human capacities invariably fuse into a discernible identity that makes that organization unique.

"I am unique,"

III. THE LAW OF CONSTANCY
Identity is fixed, transcending time and place, while its manifestations are constantly changing.

"and I am immutable, even as I grow and evolve."

IV. THE LAW OF WILL
Every organization is compelled by the need to create value in accordance with its identity.

"To truly live, however, I must express myself fully,"

V. THE LAW OF POSSIBILITY
Identity foreshadows potential.

"and in this regard, I have much to give."

VI. THE LAW OF RELATIONSHIP
Organizations are inherently relational, and those relationships are only as strong as the natural alignment between the identities of the participants.

"But to do so, I need others, and am most productive with those who need me in return."

VII. THE LAW OF COMPREHENSION

The individual capacities of an organization are only as valuable as the perceived value of the whole of that organization.

> *"To establish these relationships I must first be recognized for who I am,"*

VIII. THE LAW OF THE CYCLE

Identity governs value, which produces wealth, which fuels identity.

> *"and it follows then that I will receive in accordance with what I give."*

Taken together, the Laws of Identity largely abolish traditional distinctions between "leadership" and "management," laying out in their place a path for all to follow—for individuals who simply want to make the most of their unique capacities, and for managers bent on having their companies do the same. Call it simply *identity-based management.* Because the Laws of Identity remove the wall between "managers" and "leaders," I use these two words interchangeably throughout this book.

No life can be lived to the fullest, no organization can hope to reach its potential, without first embracing the Laws of Identity. In the end, the laws are totally interdependent and inseparable. Each, however, has its own special story to tell and lessons to impart—secrets, as it were—about management in times of change for individuals and organizations alike.

In presenting the story of identity-based management, I have called upon my experience with numerous companies that have wrestled with change and growth. Equally important, however, I have drawn on my own life as the human counterpoint to the business narrative. I have done this for three reasons:

- First, because the Laws of Identity are drawn directly from human experience and need a human frame of reference in order to be fully appreciated. It is imperative to see the connection the Laws provide between one's self as business executive (or, in my case, professional) and one's self as simply "one's self."

- Second, because mine is the life I know best and so constitutes the most reliable example for illustrating how the Laws of Identity affect individuals in their everyday lives.

- Third, because leadership, as prescribed by the Laws of Identity, is a state of being that is as obtainable by the common person, in relation to those whose lives he or she affects, as it is the province of the rich or famous. Where and how each of us will express leadership in our lives is unknown before the fact. But the imperative to do so is innate. Identity, along with the leadership potential it contains, is a function of simply being alive.

My aim in using my life as a reference point is to stimulate all readers to consider their own lives—their own identities—within the pages of this book, as a vital step in the process of leading, and working with, others.

1 THE LAW OF BEING

**ANY ORGANIZATION COMPOSED OF ONE
OR MORE HUMAN BEINGS IS ALIVE IN ITS
OWN RIGHT, EXHIBITING DISTINCT PHYSICAL,
MENTAL, AND EMOTIONAL CAPACITIES
THAT DERIVE FROM, BUT TRANSCEND,
THE INDIVIDUALS WHO MAKE UP THAT
ORGANIZATION OVER TIME.**

I am alive, I am unique,
> *and I am immutable,*
>> *even as I grow and evolve.*
To truly live, however, I must express myself fully,
> *and in this regard, have much to give.*
But to do so, I need others, and am most productive
> *with those who need me in return.*
To establish these relationships, I must first be
> *recognized for who I am,*
>> *and it follows then that*
I will receive in accordance with what I give.

I had always assumed I was alive because, like all individuals, I breathed, forged relationships, and made my way in the world. It wasn't until I was twenty-seven that I realized that up until that point, I had unknowingly confused *living* with merely *existing*.

When I was four years old, I underwent eye surgery to correct a strabismus problem—being cross-eyed. The operation was technically a success, but in the course of that operation, my life changed forever. To this day, I can recall being strapped down, alone on the operating table, watching in terror as the gas mask was brought to my face, not understanding at all what was happening. I was literally out of control. What I sensed was imminent death. At that critical moment, part of me went away. I escaped down a black hole—my "tunnel" to freedom and survival.

In that second, when I had eluded the grasp of the unknown man above me in the green mask, it seemed like a point of no return. But at the instant I slipped away, in the midst of absolute terror, I made a vow to myself that I would return. *I would be back.* Since that day I have been at work—more unconsciously than consciously—to restore my integrity as a whole individual.

Twenty-three years later, on September 2, 1977, I signed into Yale–New Haven Hospital at 1 o'clock in the morning to prepare for a corneal transplant in my right eye. The surgeon reassured me that all would be well and that later that morning I would have better vision than I had had in recent years. As I listened to his words, I knew that there was far more at stake in the next few hours than just my ability to engage the world through sharper eyes.

I awoke some six hours later with an intensely vibrant sense of self. What I saw with my "new eye," on the sunlit brick wall outside my window, was the image of the child who had all but gone away twenty-three years before: I had reclaimed a part of my self.

In those first few shimmering moments after I awakened following surgery, I could see more clearly than I had ever seen before. Everything had a freshness I could not have imagined only a day earlier. Everything seemed startlingly new. Emotionally, too, something was happening to me. I felt free of old fears—fears about losing my job, of my father's unpredictable anger, of not being the obedient child. In that moment, I was unfettered by my past. As much as this operation had helped to restore my vision, it also had restored my sense of being in control and a level of self-confidence that had been all but lost years ago.

I lay there and felt, for the first time in my life, that I had a choice: to live or simply to exist. The former path meant pursuing what *I* believed was important and right. The latter meant continuing just to do what others expected of me.

When it comes to people, the Law of Being speaks to the need for separation from all others as a prerequisite to understanding who you are. There is no way I could have come to understand myself if I had relied on others, directly or indirectly, to define my capabilities, set my course, or tell me what I was truly passionate about. For all their love, my parents had their agenda: expectations about who I was and what I should and shouldn't do. My friends, like all friends, were quick with advice on everything from what girl to date to which classes to take and which to avoid. College guidance counselors, some of whom became true and valued supporters, suggested erroneous career paths, as did early bosses (e.g., those at Yankelovich, Skelly & White who suggested that I consider national sales management).

One of the most obvious distinctions between people we call leaders and those we don't is that most leaders are, or at least appear to be, more dynamic, charismatic, *alive*. Whether gregarious or quiet, they speak their minds, project self-confidence, make vital decisions, and have the ability to convert others to their views. Simply to exist—to get by day to day and get along with others—isn't enough. For them, being all they are capable of being—living to the fullest—is life's challenge and an essential aspect of leadership.

It is paradoxical that the very relationships we seek and need in order to live full lives can be barriers to living in that they make demands on us and apply pressures that can, if we aren't careful, mask who we really are.

The reality for business leaders is even more dramatic. The companies they guide are generally perceived as innately rudderless. Yes, they have rich cultures that are defined by shared values, beliefs, and behaviors. And yes, they can legitimately be described as organic communities evolving over time. But the underlying assumption remains that it is the company's leaders who set its direction. The truth is not that simple.

The Law of Being calls into question the very nature of corporations. Are they designed and formed solely for purposes of profit, best managed through functional disciplines, business processes, assembly lines, and sales quotas? Or are corporations as alive as the people who work inside them, taking on human characteristics that must be acknowledged if these organizations are to thrive? This seemingly philosophical question isn't philosophical at all; it is sharply practical. For if the latter is the case, then the challenge of leadership gets turned on its head: Instead of the leader, whether a CEO or general manager, directing the institution, *it is the institution that directs the leader*, laying out before him or her a timeless path to value creation based on the institution's identity.

A TIME FOR CHANGE

The mid-eighties were a restless time for me. I was, on the one hand, deeply content with my professional life in identity consulting. Anspach Grossman Portugal's practice was a window on the world; I traveled extensively and worked with high-powered managers on fascinating assignments. At the same time, I was feeling constrained. I felt tied to conventional methods of problem solving. In the course of a year or two, I had come to see that corporate identity, in terms of both theory and practice, was a field open to far greater exploration than had taken place to date. Knowing this haunted me. I needed to break out. I needed a platform to grow.

By the spring of 1985, I had been with AGP for four and a half years and had advised a variety of American and overseas companies on identity-related issues. These issues ranged from name changes to corporate repositioning, most often in the wake of mergers, acquisitions, and restructurings. I had had the opportunity to work with Electronic Data Systems under the direction of Ross Perot; to help "give birth" to National Australia Bank, the result of a merger down under between two rival banks; to assist BOC Health Care, the world medical equipment and anesthetic pharmaceuticals business of the former BOC Group; and to serve Fidelity Investments as Ned Johnson, III drove his financial services locomotive relentlessly forward.

The assignment with Fidelity in particular had opened my eyes to the hidden power of identity—specifically, the power of identity to shape the fortunes of an organization beyond the surface impact of image and reputation. Emerging from my experience with Fidelity, I determined that it was time to step out on my own in the world of identity consulting.

In April 1985, along with two other partners, I founded Identica. It was a venture that, in hindsight, can be best described as a platform for pushing the envelope of identity consulting. It was a time of experimentation—of developing, testing, and refining tentative theories about the true nature and role of corporate identity.

One of the things that burned in my mind as we set up our new firm was the prospect of dissecting the idea that the whole is greater than the sum of its parts. I had turned this phrase over in my head hundreds of times, using it regularly with clients in describing how their identity captured something more than just the various business lines, products, and divisions that made up the visible fabric of the company. *The whole is greater than the sum of its parts.* It was one of those elegant expressions that everyone had come to accept, but to me, it still begged for clarification. What, exactly, was "the whole"? This question caused me to think once again about whether companies were rudderless entities, formed solely for purposes of profit, or as human—as alive—as the people within them.

Whatever nagging doubts I may have had about the answer to this question dissolved in the period 1986 through 1987. It was then that I worked with Alcoa, as chief executive Charles Parry and his team sought to broaden the scope of the business beyond aluminum.

ALCOA

Cleveland Facility, June 1986

I have visited many manufacturing facilities over the years and have seen acres and acres of land that have been converted into roofed cities of steel, concrete, and glass. I am still moved by the incredible scale of these operations and by the thousands of people who, often by night as well as day, live their work lives between those myriad walls. What impresses me is the choreography of it all—the exquisite integration of people and machinery that generates societal improvements as well as corporate profits.

In June of 1986 it was already August-hot, a situation that intensified my response as I toured the Cleveland smelting and forging facility. Visiting the site was a crucial part of getting to know Alcoa as one of the world's leading aluminum producers. The plant was bustling during my two-hour visit.

Toward the end of the tour, I was escorted along a steel and wire balcony that must have run a straight quarter-mile along the edge of a room that contained a number of giant furnaces. Two were in operation, pouring molten aluminum into forging molds several feet below their lips. It was an unforgettable sight. Despite my distance from the furnaces, I could feel the heat press against my suit and the hard-hat and goggles I wore. The metal was white-hot as it cascaded into the molds below. Thousands of sparks flew around the edges like fireworks escorting the aluminum. It was essential Alcoa. What I thought of then wasn't the cooling baths that followed or the extrusion and cutting process. What I pictured were Boeing 747s, conductor cable, semiconductor chip housings, armor plating, Tetra-Paks®, aluminum siding, pots and pans, and Coke cans—all shaped, molded, and wrapped in "Alcoa."

In that room, I was watching a portion of America's gross domestic product being born. There is almost no sector of the economy that goes untouched by the tons of molten metal that were racing along that manufacturing path on their way to becoming something of value to society.

Like many large, upstream corporations, Alcoa was largely unfamiliar to the general public. It was one of those companies that focuses chiefly on exploring for, and producing, oil and minerals or on fabricating these materials into basic products such as metals, chemicals, and plastics that go into everything from conductor cable and airplane skins to test tubes and clothing materials. Alcoa is a company whose outsized impact on society is generally unrecognized by the majority of people whose lives are profoundly affected by its efforts.

As I would soon discover, all the might that was on display in that Cleveland plant that hot June afternoon was nothing compared to the power that resided within Alcoa itself, a corporate being that was hell-bent on shaping the world it served.

In the fall of 1985, about six months after Identica opened its doors, an article appeared in the *New York Times* business section that featured Alcoa and its search for diversification. It included a picture of Charles Parry, then CEO, looking hard into the distance. I could see that this was a man determined to diversify and, I hoped, one who might welcome a chance to understand better the potential that resided within the organization as a whole.

I figured the best way to get the ball rolling was to state my case directly in a letter. About two weeks later I received an invitation to meet with Dick Fischer, senior vice president and the company's general counsel. It was a critical moment for Identica. We were only a few months old, but I sensed we were about to sign up a very big client.

Shortly after our meeting in Pittsburgh, we were engaged by Fischer to help management pave the way for change. The belief was that the identity of Alcoa was in transition as a result of diversification and that redefining and communicating the "new Alcoa" would be an important part of building support for change, internally and externally. In the end, it was an assignment that would wind up clarifying for me the governing influence of identity on an organization's ability not only to change, but also to lead its market and alter society.

It was Dick Fischer whose intellectual curiosity fueled the assignment and who became a colleague in the name of discovery. As he made clear to us in numerous ways, he wanted to "know the identity of Alcoa."

Dick had a twinkle in his eye that was never dimmed. He had an exuberance about the subject of identity that I have rarely encountered in a client. One day in early winter, I arrived in Pittsburgh to interview him. This was one of the first of many executive interviews we would conduct as we went about the business of discerning the identity of an enterprise that was almost literally wrapped up in its own glory: Everything in Alcoa's headquarters building that could be made from aluminum was! I recall in particular the aluminum elevators. They gave off a low-gloss sheen that surrounded their riders and eloquently expressed the conviction that Aloca's people (they often referred to themselves as "Alcoans") had about the boundless potential of the business they were in.

As Dick's assistant ushered me into his office, I found him staring out his window at a view that stretched well beyond the limits of the city. He turned to me with a wry smile and pointed toward the horizon. He asked me if I knew the story about two bricklayers, each of whom was regarding a pile of bricks. Dick didn't wait for my response but continued. When asked what he saw, the first man, after staring at the pile, replied with consternation that he saw just that—a pile of bricks. The second tradesman raised his eyes to his questioner and said in measured tones that what he saw was a cathedral. Fischer's message was clear: Was Alcoa simply a collection of assets or was there more to the enterprise than met the eye?

In the course of our interview, Dick indicated that he saw identity as the channel that connected the institution to the world outside. Although the assignment we were given focused on helping management better communicate impending changes born of diversification, Fischer's unspoken aim was broader: He wanted to know what, if anything, lay behind the aluminum curtain. He wanted to know what made Alcoa *Alcoa*.

A Time to Stretch

The mid-to-late 1980s could be characterized as a period of vigorous exploration and trial and error for Alcoa. When I began consulting to the company, Charles Parry and company president Fred Fetteroff were already taking steps to meet new economic and competitive pressures. In relation to the core aluminum business, one goal was to shrink, but strengthen, activities in response to industry consolidation. For instance, Alcoa was looking to reduce smelting capacity by 25%. At the same time, the company was continuing its search for new, significant uses for aluminum in industrial and commercial products that would have broad market potential. Along these lines, Alcoa had invested $142 million that year to stimulate technological innovation directed at higher-value-added applications. Packaging systems, where aluminum could offer an advantage in terms of cost, flexibility, and dependability, were a hot item at the time.

Another exciting initiative was the pursuit of acquisitions and mergers designed to broaden the company's business beyond aluminum. Few hard and fast rules guided these initiatives, other than the need to meet stipulated rates of return. Internal business probes, such as new-product development in the core aluminum business and partnership ventures with outsiders, were under way. The aim was to develop new technologies, products and markets in areas such as ceramics and separations—deriving new materials from taking apart existing ones.

These "micro" initiatives were complemented by others that were clearly macro in scope and ambition. I recall one conversation with Dick Fischer, who indicated that Alcoa was considering the acquisition of a major aerospace and defense company, that talks were "very serious," and that if it came to fruition, the deal would fundamentally reshape Alcoa. In the end, the purchase never came off. But in my eyes, that wasn't the point. In 1986, mega-deals on this scale were rare. For management even to have contemplated such a massive acquisition was, I sensed, classic Alcoa—an expression of the enormous passion for aluminum, and its boundless uses, that pulsed through the veins of this seemingly conservative metals and manufacturing enterprise.

As I sat and listened to Dick describe the other company, I could sense what he must have felt: *It would be a great fit. It would move Alcoa farther downstream, expanding even more broadly Alcoa's powerful influence in terms of proprietary technology and large-scale product development.*

My official task was to develop a positioning strategy for Alcoa, which started with articulating what made the organization distinctive.

In many ways this was standard fare: For years, corporate positioning has been accepted practice for clients and consultants alike. But it has never been standard fare to me. Each such assignment has been an opportunity for discovery, a chance to drill deep into the bedrock of the company in order to identify the unique characteristics that define identity. Such was the case with Alcoa.

Identity analysis is governed by the process of deconstruction followed by reconstruction. Everything is taken apart and then put back together again in a way that addresses the whole of the organization. Everything is geared to answering the question *How does this organization create proprietary value?*

What must be analyzed? What are the inputs that managers must consider? There are many, but three stand out. First are the experiences, behaviors, and perceptions of those stakeholders who are directly involved in the value creation process, among them managers and employees, customers, investors, and suppliers. In each case, it is a matter of analyzing the relationship that exists in order to articulate how the company creates proprietary value for that particular group.

Of high importance, as well, is corporate history, especially for organizations but have been around for decades, time having allowed them to deepen and refine their identities. A third valuable source of information and insight is company literature, executive speeches, existing market research, and other published materials. These can be read between the lines, as well as taken at face value, for useful clues to the nature of the institution.

Above all, discerning identity is about *seeing through* all the layers: through the products and services that fill brochures, store shelves, assembly lines, and loading docks; through the organizational units (the business unit, divisions, departments, and offices) that house employees; through the tenets of culture that prescribe rules of behavior; through the economic assumptions about "what business we're in"—through all of this until you reach down to the heart, mind, and soul of the company as a self-directing entity in the purest sense. This is where identity lies, moving to its own rhythm, unencumbered by all the layers that distract managers from what really "makes the company tick." Put in other terms, it is like standing on top of a mountain, looking around for signs of life, when all along that life is right under one's feet. For every leader in search of identity, it is there to be found, but only by taking the time to look down.

The challenge of unearthing Alcoa's identity in the face of diversification was great. If I hadn't been careful, all the attention being paid to diversification beyond aluminum could easily have led me off course. And discerning identity was even harder because efforts to diversify—to build Alcoa—were accompanied by management's simultaneous attempts to decentralize—to *de*integrate the company. I sensed the tension that these combined forces were producing, and I weighed their possible effects on the identity of the enterprise. The right type of diversification, I reasoned, could strengthen Alcoa, assuming that the avenues management took proved to be in sync with identity. Decentralization, however, could serve to hobble the productive power of Alcoa if it went too far; it could undermine critical cross-divisional and cross-functional relationships that served to reinforce Alcoa's identity.

The stated aim of decentralization was to enhance employee performance, foster a more market-driven orientation, and locate operating responsibility close to the customer through direct profit-and-loss accountability at the business unit level. For managers longing for greater autonomy, this was to be a golden age. But for the vast majority of employees, it was a time of exquisite confusion. Everything seemed to be up for grabs: the composition of the business, how it was organized, even, implicitly, the perceived worth of its proud heritage, so much of which stemmed from the Hall Process—the pioneering technology of the enterprise.

The Hall Miracle

I have found that every organization has in its history an event, an experience, or a moment that is the crucible in which its modern identity is formed. In Alcoa's case, this experience was the Hall Process. The Hall Process wasn't just the result of a scientific experiment; it was an act that defied the scientific odds, the financial odds, and the business odds. It was impossible to investigate the identity of Alcoa without studying the Hall Process and how it came to be. Not simply because of the central role it played in liberating aluminum—making it commercially viable—but because so many of the managers I spoke with referred to it as more than just a piece of history.

In a chemistry class at Oberlin College in 1883, Charles Martin Hall apparently heard his teacher, Professor Frank F. Jewett, talk about aluminum and about the difficulty of finding a way to prepare it economically. Reportedly, Jewett said, "Any person who discovers a process by which aluminum can be made on a commercial scale will bless humanity and make a fortune for himself." Charles Hall decided to take up the challenge. It wouldn't be easy. Beyond having to come up with the right formula for producing aluminum, Hall had to build his own apparatus and mix his own chemicals; there was no precedent for his work. Professor Jewett became Hall's mentor, challenging him to succeed. He also provided laboratory facilities, materials, and current knowledge of chemistry.

On February 23, 1886, Charles Hall produced globules of aluminum metal by the electrolysis of aluminum oxide dissolved in a cryolite-aluminum fluoride mixture. It was, for its time, close to a miracle of chemistry. Hall had beaten the scientific odds, and the rewards for doing so were potentially his.

Shortly after his successful experiment, Hall formed the Pittsburgh Reduction Company, the predecessor to Alcoa. First, however, he had to survive the defection of two Boston backers and an attempt by the Cowles Electric Smelting and Aluminum Company to suppress his new process by buying him out. He also had to stand his ground in the face of a challenge to his patent rights by the French scientist, Paul Heroult, who had filed his own patent for a similar process. Charles Hall won. Soon this new metal, aluminum, was on it way to changing how the world worked.

In reflecting on how the Hall Process affected Alcoa's identity, I realized that this "process" was as much about liberating businesses and lives as about freeing aluminum from its mineral confines. I now better understood the potency of aluminum as the icon of the company. I also better appreciated the risks inherent in advocating non-aluminum avenues of diversification without explaining how those avenues might provide socioeconomic benefits as well.

What would emerge as Alcoa's center of gravity if aluminum took a back seat to other materials? How would Alcoa continue to contribute to society? These were the urgent questions that weighed on managers' minds, sometimes publicly, sometimes not. Addressing these questions constituted a core leadership challenge for Charles Parry and his team.

In one discussion, a middle manager remarked that Alcoa was decentralizing so much that he wouldn't be surprised if the janitor became his own business unit. Humor aside, it struck me that this comment signaled this man's deep fear that decentralization threatened the integrity of the enterprise. He simply wasn't prepared for the disassembling of an institution that had, as he put it, "gotten rich" by focusing its collective efforts on increasing the productivity of customers and society for over a hundred years.

As I discovered in the course of conducting interviews, Identica had been engaged in part because a number of executives feared that when the dust had settled—after the company had been fully decentralized—there would be little left that one could actually call Alcoa. The need for identity had become an unofficial agenda item for management.

In many ways, Alcoa was an early adopter of the elixir we refer to today as "change." But it came at a cost that intensified the need to understand identity from the outset. I found that change, for all its inherent business logic, had become an agent of uncertainty, rather than of confidence, in the company's future. Anxiety about decentralization and diversification gnawed relentlessly at the foundation of what Alcoa was supposedly all about: taking aluminum in its rawest form and turning it into material that makes it easier and safer for people to live their lives.

Internally, the uncertainty that change fostered had reached the point where any consensus around corporate mission had evaporated— this in a company that had thrived for over a century on the strength of one mission: *to be the best aluminum company in the world.*

One thing that became crystal clear to me through my involvement with Alcoa is that no company that aspires to lead its market or its industry can hope to do so without a mission that binds the welfare of the institution to the welfare of society in some concrete and material way. A company's identity at once supplies and explains that bond.

Forging and communicating this bond is what fires employees' passion to succeed in good times and bad and lends meaning to their work that far transcends money alone. I realized that if Charles Parry was going to succeed in selling his organization on the merits of diversification, he would have to make this connection clear.

For all the passion that fueled Alcoa's long-standing mission, it simply didn't pass this crucial test. Being "the best aluminum company in the world" didn't go far enough; it failed to articulate Alcoa's impact on customers and society. As a result, it left employees without an anchor to steady them as they faced a sea of change.

The "I" Emerges

Alcoa was more than a business; it was a dynamic, complex being that defied simple explanations of what made it special. As I made my way through the company, it was easy to get lost in the thicket of diversification, technologies, operations, customer relationships, corporate history, and culture that were the most obvious elements of its strategy, infrastructure, and organization.

If there was any way to discern Alcoa's identity, it was to slice through these familiar business markers and answer a key question: If you strip away what the organization makes and sells (in this case aluminum), and if you regard the 55,000 employees as one individual, then what is it that this particular "individual" is really good at? What are the unique skills, expertise, and talents that that individual has honed over the past hundred years?

It was a question deliberately designed to reveal how Alcoa created value, *proprietary value*. As much as it was a "business" question, however, its power was drawn from the strength of how we, as human beings, operate.

As I have learned through personal experience and by observing others, an individual's identity—the unique characteristics that make each of us special—is the source of the value we are capable of creating in our respective worlds. This is evident whether we measure our contribution in terms of the health of our business, the strength of our family, or the welfare of our community. The same holds true for organizations.

A company's identity is the source of the value *it* is capable of creating in its world. Value creation is where business and life converge. It is the "way in" to the realm of identity, the path to knowing who we really are, and what we truly stand for. For this reason, I have come to rely totally on understanding the dynamics of value creation as the foundation for discovering identity. The challenge is to find the patterns, recurrences, similarities in how the organization works that reveal the story of value creation.

Beyond Aluminum

Identity can be elusive, the process of discovery subtle. As I noted earlier, certain steps are routine: conducting in-depth interviews with internal and external constituencies, performing content analysis of corporate and marketing literature, between-the-lines readings of executive speeches, and probing reviews of corporate history.

I have also found that there is often a step that needs to be taken that isn't always obvious at the beginning. In Alcoa's case, that step was a close analysis of three functions that were at the center of Alcoa's value creation process: research and development, engineering, and sales and marketing. I reasoned that if I could clarify and then link together the particular contributions of each of these functions, a clearer picture of the whole might emerge.

My assessment of these three key functions was revealing. R&D's contribution came in the form of new materials—what amounted to new building blocks that Alcoa could use to shape its future. For all its sophistication, the R&D process contained its own alchemy, not unlike the original Hall Process. It focused on the process of separation, taking apart existing materials to create new ones—among them membranes— and new adsorption technologies. R&D worked with ceramics, including powder processing, carbo-thermics, and plasma. The development of new alloys, such as aluminum lithium, magnesium lithium, and the company-branded Alcoa Alloy 6009, were research priorities, as was the creation of composites, such as Arall 1. The process of creation was alive and well within Alcoa's research and development function.

The effects of engineering were readily apparent. Alcoa's deep engineering skills had contributed inestimably to the design and production of new industrial, commercial, defense, and consumer products. These included airplanes, conductor cable, automobiles, bridge decks, packages, armor plate, chip housings, and even home siding and cookware.

The products themselves, however, didn't tell the whole story. If there was magic at Alcoa—and in many ways there was—it existed within the engineering discipline. As I studied this vital function, I felt compelled to take a look at the literal meaning of engineering; I needed to know more. What I learned illuminated the significance of this function and the importance of keeping it intact. According to *Webster's*, engineering is "an applied science concerned with utilizing inorganic products of earth, properties of matter, sources in nature, and physical forces for supplying human needs in the form of structures, machines, manufactured products, precision instruments and industrial organization. It is the means of lighting, heating, refrigeration, communications, transportation, sanitation and public safety and other productive work." Not *a* means of doing these things, *the* means. Engineering was Alcoa's center of gravity. Its definition revealed the company's connection with society.

Alcoa was also very good at marketing and sales. As a consequence of the organization's long-standing regard for the societal, as well as the economic, value of aluminum, Alcoa managers had turned customer education and conversion into art forms. The genesis of this vital skill could be traced back to the roots of the company.

As part of my analysis, I read the book *Alcoa: An American Enterprise*. It was the company's official history, and it contained numerous lines that revealed Alcoa's early commitment to, and success at, marketing in the broadest sense:

Nobody wanted the new metal in the beginning. . . . Alcoa had to pioneer the new uses.

Making satisfactory tubing at a reasonable cost proved to be a long and tedious process. A market acceptance had to be created at the same time.

The company had to go into the manufacture of sheet, cable, extruded and forged shapes, wire, rod, bar, castings, foil, powder and paste, and screw machine products.

It had to go even further into the manufacture of cooking utensils, bottle caps, and aluminum furniture.

It is revealing today, in this time we refer to as the knowledge age or the information age, to look back at the dynamics of Alcoa's marketing and sales process. In many ways, Alcoa managers and employees had already figured it out: They built customer support by effectively "packaging" knowledge as a means of establishing authority in a field (aluminum). They did this by developing an exhaustive library of customer education materials that, as was evident in visits to customers' offices, dominated the book shelves—and therefore the minds—of these vital individuals.

Cracking the code of Alcoa's identity was like putting together a thousand-piece jigsaw puzzle; all of the pieces were there, but how they fit together was not at all obvious. It wasn't until nearly the end of my analysis that the pieces came together into a unified, logical picture of the whole.

I was in the middle of an employee focus group in Pittsburgh. A product manager in the packaging division kept harping on technology. With unusual intensity, he stressed that Alcoa had always been "good at" technology, but now, with all this attention devoted to change and the planned dispersing of its centralized engineering function, he feared that the company's technological skills, developed largely around aluminum applications, would be left behind.

These words triggered a crucial insight for me. *Change*, I thought. Change had taken on a negative aura for many people, who saw it as a threat to the identity of Alcoa as they had come to understand it: simply as an aluminum company. But change actually represented the greatest clue of all in unearthing the identity of the corporation. I revisited the evaluation I had just completed of Alcoa's R&D, engineering, and sales and marketing functions, making connections among technical innovation, product development, and customer conversion. What I realized was that the sum of the effects of these functions held the seeds of Alcoa's identity.

What distinguished Alcoa as a business institution—aluminum just happened to be the metal involved—was its *genius for transformation*. Not transformation in the popular sense of corporate change, but transformation as a comprehensive applied "science" that, as I soon understood, included four interdependent stages: *technological transformation, product transformation, market transformation, and societal transformation*. Alcoa, *the individual*, was driven by its singular ability to manage the process of transformation as a discrete technology that explained how the company created value for its customers, value for society, and, in return, wealth for its shareholders (Exhibit one).

The pieces of the identity puzzle fell into place. How the various stages of transformation worked and the results they produced were fast becoming self-evident. In each instance, small, seemingly innocuous phrases I had picked up in the course of our interviews over the past three months suddenly took on new meaning.

- *Technological transformation* was prescribed by Alcoa's robust research operations and the discoveries and innovations they yielded. One of the widely accepted expressions I recall from my discussions with employees was that Alcoa had a "zest for experimentation." Within the context of technological transformation, the significance of this simple phrase was now clear.

- *Product transformation* was about liberation through engineering. It was about infusing into otherwise inert materials motion, speed, kinetic properties, and almost boundless malleability. As I put this piece of the identity puzzle into place, I remembered the words of one of Alcoa's largest industrial customers, who, as I was leaving his office, remarked, "Alcoa likes to turn rocks into rockets."

- *Market transformation* was a natural offshoot of Alcoa's skill at product transformation. The process was a science in its own right. It worked like this: Alcoa would envision a new application for aluminum, acquaint the customer with its infinite benefits, and persuade the customer to try it. This invariably led to substitution. The results have manifested themselves in markets great and small, glamorous and humble. Consider the shift from airplanes wrapped in fabric to those clothed in aluminum, from wood siding to aluminum siding, from steel beverage cans to aluminum ones. Commenting to me in an early interview, a commercial customer made it clear that the more he and his company knew about aluminum, the better off their business was. Reflecting on his relationship with Alcoa, he said, "Alcoa educates you to pieces."

- *Societal transformation* worked as follows: On the strength of having invented or expanded a given market, people adopted and accepted new ways of living and doing business. Most often, the large-scale changes Alcoa inspired had a universal impact, setting new standards and opening opportunities for virtually everyone. The gradual, steady shift from railroads to air transportation is a prime example. Alcoa's efforts produced shorter travel times and enabled people to get to places that had been unreachable before. Societal transformation was the desired result for Alcoa; it was the end game. In the words of one customer, "Alcoa had made aluminum a catalyst of change for America."

Alcoa's enormous impact on society had crystallized for me a vital fact: *value flows upstream.* No matter where a company is in the value chain—whether it is a provider of raw materials, a fabricator or manufacturer, a distributor or service organization—its identity draws its strength from the contribution it makes to the life and well-being of the

EXHIBIT ONE

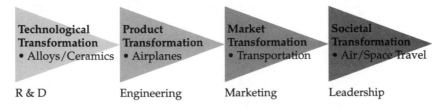

Technological Transformation	Product Transformation	Market Transformation	Societal Transformation
• Alloys/Ceramics	• Airplanes	• Transportation	• Air/Space Travel
R & D	Engineering	Marketing	Leadership

Value Creation Path

end-user. Understanding and investing in this relationship, no matter how far removed the company may see itself from the end-user, is the only way to ensure the on-going relevance and growth of the enterprise.

From this vantage point, the headwaters of value creation aren't at the point of raw materials sourcing and production, or engineering and manufacturing; they rest with society, which is where human needs and desires are born. It is only in working its way back "upstream," and comprehending its distinctive contribution to society, that a company can come to know and capitalize on its true potential for value creation.

For Alcoa, aluminum amounted to a metal prism through which the company passed its extraordinary beam of light—its genius for transformation—in an effort to create value in forms that only it was capable of delivering. All of Alcoa—its past, present, and future, its successes and failures, its investment decisions, its culture and operating priorities—could be better understood in light of its identity. Understanding that identity brought into sharp relief the value-creating capacities of the corporation that had remained hidden before.

Most striking of all was how Alcoa's genius for transformation operated independent of current management. In many ways, it even stood apart from the 55,000 employees who at that time populated the company. The identity of Alcoa, as I saw it, was not a product of the moment, of its current CEO, or even of the past several years. It had formed generations earlier, deepening and becoming more complex with time.

It was the discovery of Alcoa's genius for transformation that led me to see that this company was literally alive—a self-directing being with a mind of its own. What other conclusion could be drawn when the evidence pointed to a 100-year history, along with current events, which could be explained so completely by a single statement of fact? In that moment I realized, as I had sensed in my work with other companies before, that no organization, no corporate *being*, could exhibit such a unique, all-encompassing capacity and *not* be alive in its own right.

Impossible as it may be to prove scientifically, I have found that all organizations contain a palpable life force that is born of, yet stands apart from, the employees who people it over time. Indirectly, psychoanalyst Carl Jung alludes to this "life force" in terms of the collective unconscious. Jung describes the collective unconscious as "an echo of the sum of experience accessible to all humans, that manifests itself through archetypes or patterns of expression, that acquire strength through repetition." *Strength through repetition.* In business circles, this life force and the strength it contains are implied routinely in references to institutional knowledge and institutional memory.

That organizations are living, self-directing beings is a phenomenon of nature that contains its own common-sense logic: Putting together two or more human beings to achieve a common goal (build a business, make money, solve a problem) necessarily yields something larger in terms of mind and spirit than a mere collection of individuals. For example, William Hewlett and David Packard gave birth to Hewlett-Packard, an institution with a distinct sense of identity that is both the long shadow of its founders and unique in its own right.

The particular capacities that define the identities of different people blend, fuse, and deepen over time into an identity all their own, the identity of the organization. Like the human beings whose special needs, drive, and talent fueled the company initially, the organization—*the corporate being*—seeks to follow its own path in order to realize its innate potential. The dynamics of the human being and the dynamics of an organization are one and the same. Physical, mental, and emotional capacities define individuality in one, just as in the other.

But what does this mean about the uniqueness of the people who are part of the company? Does their individuality simply disappear in the shadow of the enterprise? On the contrary. A corporation's identity *affirms* the uniqueness of all the human beings who are, have been, or will be the fabric of the organization. How is this so? Organizations are self-selecting beings, keeping some people while rejecting others. What the organization is "selecting" are those people whose unique characteristics add weight and depth to its own. Corporate identity celebrates individual identity. When people are aligned with the right organization, they are liberated to be who they naturally are.

In conceiving of Alcoa as an individual, I was able to "read" the organization in terms of its particular physical, mental, and emotional capacities. Its physical composition, for instance, showed in the company's powerful mining, smelting, and refining operations, as well as in its many other facilities and overall infrastructure. Its mental, or cognitive vigor was manifest in the managers' intellectual creativity, which had spawned the ideas and initiatives that were driving diversification. The Hall Process and Alcoa's renowned engineering competence also stood as examples of the company's cognitive strengths. Alcoa's emotional drive was readily visible on a number of levels: a passion for aluminum that employees defended with religious fervor when faced with the prospect of diversification beyond aluminum, and employees' unfettered pride in the contribution the company had made not only to its customers but also, through them, to society at large.

Toward the end of the time in which I worked with Alcoa, Paul O'Neill replaced Charles Parry as CEO. His first action was to reestablish the company's commitment to aluminum. Diversification, coupled with decentralization, was putting undue pressure on the enterprise both financially and in terms of morale. From where I sat, these two paths were getting in the way of the institution's ability to lead in the marketplace, as it had for a century.

In hindsight, it is clear that Parry's drive to diversify held great promise. It had the potential to open up avenues of growth through materials science that were natural extensions of the company's innate genius for transformation, irrespective of the material at hand. In many ways, Alcoa's identity had the potential to provide the company's leadership with a roadmap for diversification. *Alcoa is alive. What are the unique characteristics that shape its identity? What is the value-creating potential inherent in this identity? What opportunities exist to realize this potential—in effect, to live in accordance with identity?* In its own way, Paul O'Neill's decision to recommit the company to aluminum acknowledged Alcoa's identity, but in far different terms: It affirmed the roots from which that identity was born.

Since 1987, Alcoa has done well. Revenues have nearly doubled, from $7.7 billion to $13.3 billion ten years later. Net income has quadrupled over the same period, growing from $200 million to over $800 million. I remain convinced, however, that this performance could have been even better, not simply in financial terms, but also in terms of Alcoa's capacity to create even greater value for society and to grow profitably as a result.

A VIEW TO LEADERSHIP

The assignment with Alcoa was a milestone that served to confirm for me the existence of identity and its profound effect on the life and welfare of organizations. I had begun to sense that certain features characterized companies like Alcoa—companies I instinctively thought of as leaders. I needed to know exactly what those features were. If I was able to discern them, they would, I felt, supply important clues about the nature of leadership.

As I went through the process of articulating these traits, I reviewed the twenty-plus corporations I had served over the past several years, trying to figure out what, if anything, they had in common. It was easily a six-month process. Finally, I homed in on three areas that seemed to capture what I had observed. The first had something to do with how well synchronized an organization was. The second area was related to how comfortable a company seemed to be with its basic or core business and how all of the parts contributed to the whole. The third area involved longevity and maturity—had the company survived crises and come out intact, if not stronger? Shortly after identifying these three general areas, I distilled each into what I saw were the features I had only sensed months earlier.

The features I detected were these. First, there was what I term *grand efficiency*. Not efficiency in operations alone, but the efficiency that comes with all parts of the enterprise working in sync. The second feature was *integrity,* in the sense of wholeness or completeness, that allows for business diversity while reinforcing the economic and social value of the institution. The third feature I discerned among these leading organizations was *endurance*. In wrestling over the years with identity issues, I had recognized that one of the chief tasks managers face is helping their companies perform while positioning them to endure over time. This fact led me to see the unique challenge—moreover, the unique opportunity—that companies have:

Unlike people, organizations face the very real prospect of enduring in perpetuity.

How these three features—grand efficiency, integrity, and endurance—coincide with organizations such as Alcoa kept running through my mind, leading me to recall an earlier conversation with Dick Fischer. In that conversation we discussed the many ramifications of Alcoa's identity—how, as Dick suggested, it constituted an "authentic" leadership platform for top management, or, possibly, a way of selling employees on change by easing the perceived threat to Alcoa's heritage. Dick commented, in passing, that the whole of Alcoa was certainly greater than the sum of its parts. Of course, I was reminded of my intense curiosity about that expression some eighteen months earlier, as Identica was opening its doors. It was now clear what "the whole" referred to.

One of the most potent concepts in business today is whole-system thinking. It refers to taking a comprehensive view of an organization, looking at it, and (more important) managing it in an integrated way. Its people, infrastructure, financial resources, business units and even the intellectual capital that weaves throughout—all are integral parts of the enterprise.

As useful as this concept is as an approach to management, I am convinced that whole-system thinking is better comprehended as whole-*being* thinking, as looking upon the organization as an individual alive in its own right. This distinction enlarges the landscape for understanding corporations and prescribing a course of action that maximizes their leadership potential.

If there is a first step in this regard, it is for managers to acknowledge that the life of their institution, as expressed by its identity, is an independent force. To date, I have found a handful of people—senior executives as well as rank-and-file employees—who have accepted this core tenet of the first Law of Identity. In so doing, they have found a new way of approaching the business of general management.

For instance, the Law of Being suggests that the things companies do on a day-to-day basis—from making investment decisions to performing routine activities such as customer calls, sales force communications, and training and development—are actually, or *should* be, the operational manifestations of *who* the company is, as defined by its identity.

Another corollary of the Law of Being is that attempts to change culture aren't always the answer to business challenges such as ensuring the success of mergers and acquisitions. Why not? Because when it comes to fundamental change—or the failure to change—culture is governed by identity, and you can't alter the effect without knowing the cause.

In 1987, the culture of Alcoa was evident in how employees behaved when confronted with the prospect of trading aluminum for other, "foreign" materials, such as ceramics and polymers. They resisted hard and many were suspicious of diversification. Their reactions showed just how much they valued aluminum as a metal that had changed the world and made money for investors in the process. It was clear that Alcoans placed a high value on such things as innovation and invention, sustained customer relationships, and societal contribution. As I observed, however, they also put a premium on tradition, often for its own sake, and on painstaking, methodical processes that sometimes seemed to have a paralyzing effect on decision making.

Although the former values were admirable, the latter, I believed, were legitimate candidates for modification, because they limited both the company's vision and its capacity for rapid response. Given the right approach, the right incentives, and adequate time, any or all of the values that framed this culture might have been "changed." But refining and improving Alcoa's culture would not alter the corporation's identity, which had given rise to that culture in the first place.

The answer to meeting business challenges such as mergers and acquisitions doesn't automatically lie in changing corporate culture. Often, the key is to understand the underlying identities of the parties involved and assess the natural compatibility of the identities of these two corporate beings *before* taking steps to alter employee attitudes and behaviors, which are a by-product of identity.

In bringing to light the fact that all companies are alive, the Law of Being implies that this life can be described in ways that illuminate its value on multiple levels which, taken together, begin to suggest a framework for leadership:

- Its *human value,* in that this life derives from the thousands of people who make up the organization over time and, thus, is a true reflection of the organization's unique skills and expertise. For example, identity can be used to address employees' fear of change as long as that change is consonant with, and cast legitimately within the context of, identity. In Alcoa's case, Charles Parry might have explained diversification as follows: "Our genius for transformation distinguishes this company and has done so for a century. That is the nature of this institution; we are driven to transform things: products, markets, society. Aluminum was the genesis of our great talent, but it is not what makes us great. Our genius for transformation transcends the metal—and our decision to diversify is made in view of this reality. The avenues we pursue will, I assure you, be wholly in keeping with our identity."

- Its *business value,* in terms of the company's distinctive contribution in the marketplace, such as products and services that flow from and reinforce identity, or joint ventures that build upon the unique, value-creating characteristics of the partners.

- Its *societal value,* in relation to how this life force brings about social improvement, such as Alcoa's impact on transportation, energy, and food preservation.

- Its *economic value,* in terms of how the combined effects of this life are reflected in its basic financial worth, including stock price performance over time and portfolio turnover.

For managers, not to follow this first Law of Identity, the Law of Being, is to limit their companies' best efforts at value creation, for doing so ignores the innate strengths of the institution and the path they suggest. Can the designated leader—the CEO, the division head—set direction at will? Certainly, he or she can try. If such leaders are fortunate, the course they lay out will be consistent with the identity of the enterprise. But, if it isn't, the chances of success are slim. The institution seeks to lead itself. The identity of the organization is a greater, more potent force than any one individual. It knows its own potential.

All of us also have the capacity to know our own potential—to *live* rather than merely exist. It is impossible for me now to consider these four levels of value and not consider my own life within the context they provide. This first Law of Identity, and the "life" it refers to, belongs as much to me and to all individuals as it does to business organizations. Within the framework of the Law of Being, the human value of my life is measured at once by my family lineage and by my own unique capacities as an individual.

What I *do* with these special capacities is evident in the business value I create for my clients and in the social value I produce in my role as a member of my community.

Just as it does for companies, the economic value of my life provides a useful way to gauge the financial worth of how well I apply my unique strengths. At times, I have felt fairly compensated for what I do. At other times, I have felt underappreciated financially. Rather than feeling cheated, however, I have come to take that feeling as a sign that I'm not being everything I can be; in an economic sense, as in every other way, my "success" is my own responsibility.

The Law of Being demands that managers practice the art and science of value creation on all of these levels—human, business, societal, economic. Doing so calls for leaders who *liberate* identity, stewarding it and giving it room to run. The first task of all managers, then, is to understand the identity of their organization, for that identity contains the answers to questions about value creation that are impossible to find by analyzing such conventional business factors as market growth, customer attitudes, operational strengths, and technological change. Once that identity is clear, it is everyone's job to exploit these factors in ways that *serve* identity so they will become natural allies in the continual process of profitable growth through institutional achievement.

2 THE LAW OF INDIVIDUALITY

**AN ORGANIZATION'S HUMAN CAPACITIES
INVARIABLY FUSE INTO A DISCERNIBLE
IDENTITY THAT MAKES THAT ORGANIZATION
UNIQUE.**

*I am alive, **I am unique,** and I am immutable,
even as I grow and evolve.
To truly live, however, I must express myself fully,
and in this regard, have much to give.
But to do so, I need others, and am most productive
with those who need me in return.
To establish these relationships, I must first be
recognized for who I am,
and it follows then that
I will receive in accordance with what I give.*

It's one thing to know that you are alive. It's something else entirely to live according to who you are. Leaders—certainly those who seem to draw us to them effortlessly—do so. Stanley Gault, who helped revitalize Rubbermaid, and Ross Perot, who founded Electronic Data Systems, are two contemporary examples. Their authenticity as individuals shines through.

Authentic leaders exhibit that quality at all times, not just during business hours. They tend to "lead" twenty-four hours a day. For them, leadership is a way of life forged by numerous business and nonbusiness events and circumstances. Among his many exploits, Ross Perot reportedly trained horses in his youth. Did this make him a leader? Not in and of itself. But taken along with dozens of other formative experiences, some pleasant, others hard, Perot has managed to live—in business and otherwise—according to who he truly is. Doing so is the not-so-mysterious alchemy of all pied pipers.

In hindsight, I see my own life as a maze wherein I have taken several false paths. Or more precisely a jigsaw puzzle with innumerable pieces, many of which provided compelling but incomplete clues to my identity. It was close to forty years before a cogent picture emerged of what made me *me*.

As a child I loved art—in fact, anything creative—and pursued writing from an early age. I painted, enjoyed writing poems, and at the age of eight took up the guitar—classical, jazz, flamenco—which I studied and stayed with through college.

As I got closer to having to get my first full-time job, I was drawn to the business world, partly because I knew I couldn't make a living in the arts, partly because I knew that my pursuing a career in business would be far more palatable to my father. He was a classic entrepreneur—he ran three small businesses—with a great passion for the

Spanish guitar. This passion had kept us close for years, but now the rules were different; I still needed his approval and chose a course I believed would ensure me of it.

My first job out of graduate school was with AMAX in public relations in New York. An intellectually vapid assignment, it lasted six months. I returned to Boston to be with my future wife. I gravitated toward consulting, first on my own under the name the Market Development Group, then with Yankelovich, Skelly & White and with Anspach Grossman Portugal.

Above all other things, I am and will forever be an "identity consultant." Within this context, I have come to understand myself as both strategist and humanist, or, as I often think of it, as "architect" and "rabbi" dedicated to the very process of discovery and creation.

It isn't just a career issue. Rather, for me, identity is a framework for life and for living—for understanding how and why things work. This is true in my relationships with family and friends, with respect to how I have come to understand the passions of religion and the pull of political ideology, and, of course, in my interpretation of the dynamics of business organizations and their role in society.

The second Law of Identity, the Law of Individuality, poses a crucial test of leadership. Call it the test of self-knowledge. When all is said and done, this test may be the most complex, the most maddening, and yet the most comforting. There are no guideposts or "right" and "wrong" indicators to help people along the discovery path except those they erect themselves. Even so, in moments when one feels lost or uncertain, it is good to know that the answer is there to be found—that everyone has unique capacities that coalesce into a discernible identity that makes them special. It is the anchor within us all. Discerning what this identity is and how it influences others is the test every true leader must pass.

Identity is also the foundation of every business institution and a rudder in a sea of constant change. This fact was brought home to me in the fall of 1984 when I began working with Fidelity Investments. The story of Fidelity sheds light on how the Law of Individuality affects an organization's ability to become a leader in its field. This story is a window on the anatomy of differentiation.

FIDELITY INVESTMENTS

The Chart Room

For all the money that went into furnishing the office of CEO Ned Johnson III's, there was perhaps no room at Fidelity's Boston head-quarters that better captured the soul of the business than the modest chart room nearby. It was a smallish space, maybe twenty feet square, covered from top to bottom with long swaths of paper. Each chart told its own story of technical investment analysis.

Up close, I could read tea leaves by studying how the S&P average had done over the past several months, or the Dow Jones industrials, or the Russell 2000, or any number of lesser-known statistical indices that attempt to "chart" financial life. Individually, each of these charts was its own world, and each harbored a history and a lesson. The cumulative effect was almost a teasing, as though one were being dared to figure out what it all meant.

As I was being shown the room and learned how the daily charts would soon be replaced with new ones of more recent vintage, I stepped back near the door to take it all in at one time. As I moved away, it became harder and harder to make out which chart was which, and the entire room took on a different feel. The amplitudes of one chart rolled into the next. The tiny, almost imperceptible vertical volume/price lines that were the hieroglyphics of high investment became the language of the walls, a stunning, undulating wave washing in slow motion around the room.

For all the technical evaluation that went on in that room, for all the countless hours spent by countless analysts and equity managers, it seemed to me that there was a bigger point to that space than the sta-tistical messages that were being sent in the financial equivalent of Morse code. This chart room contained its own energy; it was at once understated and brilliant. Simple, even dowdy though it was , adorned largely in the blacks and whites of the printouts on the walls and the browning edges of soon-to-be-replaced charts. The chart room at Fidelity was a nerve center and, to those who understood its code, a harbinger of possible changes that would affect us all. In many ways, the room highlighted a vital aspect of Fidelity itself—passionately numerical, focused on trends, strictly rational.

The clinical nature of the chart room presented a stark contrast to the office of Ned Johnson. In my first interview with Johnson, we spoke about the future of investments, the glory of technology, and the challenges and opportunities facing Fidelity. As well as I recall Johnson's words, I recall the understated beauty and richness of the office. It was patrician and conservative. Classic oriental rugs in reds and blues were punctuated by eighteenth- and nineteenth-century antique furniture.

True power in great investment management firms resides in many quarters. I believe that in the case of Fidelity, the greatness of the firm hung neatly on a highwire between the chart room and the executive suite. Each respected the other. Each knew the other's power and would avail itself of that power often as the world of investments heated up and Fidelity shouldered its way onto the high ground of the industry.

In the days I spent interviewing Fidelity executives and roaming the halls at 161 Devonshire Street in Boston, I kept thinking about the essential difference between the chart room and Johnson's office. Both offered clues to the identity of the institution. The former was unimposing and easy to miss if you didn't know it was there: a seemingly bland landscape of ever-changing statistics. The latter was suitably well tailored and elegantly appointed in various shades of unforgettable prosperity: the apparent seat of power. Inherent in the visible contrast between these two spaces was a palpable tension. And this tension would supply a vital clue to what made Fidelity tick.

The Challenge

When I started working with Fidelity, the company's growth was already legendary, so growth *per se* was certainly not the challenge facing Ned Johnson and his management team. The challenge, as I saw it, was helping management to stay ahead of the organization in the face of its runaway success. The task was to grow with discipline and not let the institution spin out of control as its mutual funds proliferated.

One of the key requirements was to make sure that current and new investors appreciated the value in doing business with "Fidelity," and not just with its myriad funds. To do so meant delineating what made Fidelity *Fidelity*—beyond size, beyond growth rate, beyond fund performance, beyond its leading-edge use of technology. At the time we began the engagement, these challenges weren't readily apparent. They became clear as the assignment unfolded.

The Assignment

The express reason why we were called in to work with Fidelity was to help staunch the flow of investor capital that was finding its way to competitors' mutual funds groups. Investors had come to associate Fidelity primarily with an array of aggressive growth funds, and when they wanted something else (bond funds or more conservative equities), they were going elsewhere. Competitors such as T. Rowe Price and Vanguard were major beneficiaries. Fidelity customers didn't seem to realize that Fidelity offered those types of funds as well.

Ned Johnson and Fidelity's then president, Sam Bodman, were concerned about losing capital to other institutions. They needed to devise a way of holding on to hard-won investors while continuing to win new ones. The first step they took was to set a new goal for the organization: *Achieve greater customer loyalty to Fidelity, the institution, as a means of increasing depth (that is, the number of products and services used per customer) and longevity in customer relationships.*

What Fidelity's management believed was the problem—the persistent flow of customer capital to other investment houses—was, I suspected, a by-product of a larger and deeper *identity* issue. I observed immediately that managers seemed to be inattentive, at times almost grossly indifferent, to the institution itself. Instead, they paid homage to Fidelity's various funds, giving them all the glory. The "whole" of Fidelity was being lost among its parts. Each fund, under the leadership of a dynamic, entrepreneurial manager, had evolved an identity all its own. Each polished and promoted itself as though it were wholly independent of the institution. The net effect was to undermine the real as well as the perceived value of the parent, particularly in the eyes of customers who were shopping elsewhere. Ironically, as funds—the "golden eggs"—proliferated, they were slowly killing the goose that had laid them.

Clearly, no one had taken the time to figure out what it truly meant to be Fidelity beyond a collection of high-performing mutual funds. This situation constituted a void that, if left unfilled, would make management's leadership task increasingly difficult. Leading Fidelity with its high-octane, entrepreneurial fund managers and marketing executives was hard enough. Allowing the organization to continue on its growth trajectory without any sense of institutional glue to bind the whole could wind up tearing the fabric of the enterprise.

A number of managers I spoke with actively resisted the notion of a corporate entity that was greater than the sum of its parts. At times their resistance was so intense and so practiced that it seemed to have been programmed. Recalling Johnson's and Bodman's goal, it occurred to me that the hidden challenge in building loyalty to the institution was answering the question *"Loyalty to what?"* I knew from the start that what management needed to succeed meant far more than coming up with a compelling positioning statement and then translating that statement into marketing and communications programs. The "what" of Fidelity could not be fabricated. It would have to be discovered.

Cracking the Code

My investigation into Fidelity took me many places within and outside the company. It took me back into the chart room with its steadily changing reams of technical analysis; back into the beautifully appointed suites of Ned Johnson, Sam Bodman, and other Fidelity executives; into the depth and detail of carefully crafted executive speeches about "how the future would be ours"; into the not-so-random design of Fidelity's physical plant and the psychology of office allocation; and into the written history of the firm and a range of feature articles penned by ever-curious journalists. But mostly it took me into the heads and hearts of dozens of managers, employees, customers, and joint venture partners, all of whom had a vital interest in the identity of the institution—whether they were aware of it or not.

As I began my search, I looked forward to every interview and to poring over every source of knowledge that hinted at identity. Each held a clue. There was nothing random or superfluous about the questions I asked. Yet I knew that no one person I spoke to would have the answer to the question about Fidelity's identity. They were too close to the situation. In a way, each was like a single strand in the overall genetic code of the enterprise.

I began the process of deconstructing Fidelity with its culture. It was a matter of observing the behavior of executives, employees, and even customers, which had come to shape so much in terms of performance.

Fidelity's culture was defined by four pillars, or, more accurately, four passions, some more visible than others:

- The first was a commitment to private ownership. For Ned Johnson, Sam Bodman, and most of the money managers, private ownership was a passport to freedom. It was the platform for achieving independence and for maintaining maximum flexibility as a leader in the financial services business.

- The second passion revolved around innovation, or, more to the point, invention. Invention was the means of creating new and timely investment products to meet customer needs (and to create that need if it didn't already exist). Fidelity, the leader, was inventing its own future.

- Fidelity's third passion was a fierce reliance on personal skill and judgment as the foundation for building the company and managing its growth. Essentially, fund managers could place their own bets. Peter Lynch, the legendary manager of Fidelity's Magellan Fund, is the keenest example of this philosophy, given his huge bet on Chrysler stock when the auto company was on its knees in the late 1980s. Before it became fashionable in the early 1990s, empowerment was already an active ingredient in the way Fidelity's management led the institution.

- The fourth pillar was an organic, cellular structure that defied conventional organization models. Yes, there were functions, such as marketing, finance, and customer service. Yes, the bond fund department was discernible as a self-contained unit, as was equity fund management.

But what I saw was a system that was always churning and revising itself in one corner of the company or another. A new fund would open, and people would move to help sell, manage, or service this fund. The marketing executives would figure out a new and better way to manage the fulfillment process, and the organization would "resource" this process almost overnight. It was amazing to watch. Fidelity's structure was biological in nature, and it was as much cerebral as physical. Cells begot other cells. As some died or receded, new ones were born to take their place, filling the gaps—sometimes reinforcing and sometimes altering, but always maintaining, the genetic landscape.

To lead Fidelity was to lead a symphony composed of thousands of parts. To capitalize on Fidelity's cellular structure required management to balance the organization's free-wheeling, yet self-governing, genetic system with enough guidance to avoid anarchy and dysfunction.

As important as it was for me to examine culture, doing so had its limitations. During this period, my understanding of the nature of corporate identity was changing rapidly. My frame of reference for understanding uniqueness—my client's or my own—was still forming. At the time, I was deeply influenced by the thinking of Erik Erikson, a leading behaviorist whose main contribution was to bridge the gap between human development, which focuses on personal challenges, and the broader, socio-economic and cultural factors that affect us all.

As I weighed the characteristics of Fidelity, I recalled Erikson's view that people grow by successfully negotiating developmental crises. At different stages of their lives, they must achieve trust in themselves and others, autonomy, initiative, competence and productivity, and what Erikson calls "generativity"; that is, they must mold their own *identity*. Integrity and acceptance follow. The simple logic of Erikson's idea was altogether relevant to understanding what made Fidelity unique.

By this time I had come to understand that Fidelity, the institution, was *literally alive*. It engaged in a host of dynamic relationships, created and met its own challenges, dealt with crises, and continued relentlessly to grow, mature, and make its way in the world. Yet all the while, it seemed oblivious to what made it unique. Here was a great organization whose management, I sensed, was not wholly aware of the very characteristics that had made it great in the first place. "Fidelity" did not comprehend the fact of its own life. As a result, Johnson, Bodman, and their team were not capitalizing on the unique chemistry that at once explained and foreshadowed the success of the company. How, I wondered, was I going to get these managers to acknowledge not only that Fidelity was alive—a living being with a mind of its own—but also that this being had an identity as rich, vital, and self-directing as the identity of any of its employees?

The definitive power contained within this corporate being was extraordinary and could be detected on several levels: in the sheer weight of the organization, as evidenced by a steady increase in assets (from $9.5 billion in 1980 to $27 billion in 1984); through its expansive intellect, clearly evident in the steady development of a carefully screened employee population (from 800 in 1979 to over 2000 four years later); in terms of the unstoppable passion for market influence that spilled out of nearly every office (expressed by Fidelity's aggressive incursions into discount brokerage, wholesaling, and group retirement plans). The relentless development of all these physical, mental, and emotional capacities had fueled Fidelity's growth. These capacities were the true assets of leadership. But I knew that making the most of them required knowing the identity of the organization that gave rise to them, and such knowledge was conspicuous by its absence.

I was determined to fill that void and thus help make Fidelity's business strategy truly coherent. I felt that managers armed with this knowledge would be better able to align organization, culture, and operations in ways that would exploit the natural efficiency of the enterprise.

Fidelity's individuality was not defined by the actual funds and other products, services, and technology that made up the body of the organization. These factors, like culture, were manifestations of Fidelity's identity. I spent many weeks searching for clues that would help me discover what motivated this corporate being to behave the way it did.

The dynamics of fund management were a natural place to look given the funds' pivotal role in Fidelity's value creation process. Many of the traits I had discovered that defined how Johnson and Bodman led the organization—a love of independent action, reliance on personal skill and judgment, a passion for invention—were openly evident in this hotbed of activity.

Fund management relied heavily on the distinctive capabilities, insights, and actions of individual money managers. It was a mark of success that the style and approach of Fidelity's portfolio managers varied dramatically, not just between equity and bond managers but also among the equity managers themselves. Autonomy in stock selection and timing was the rule. What was good for the aggressive growth manager was "all wrong" for the equity-income manager. What made sense for Magellan was alien to the Discoverer, the Contrafund, the Mercury, and the Freedom Fund managers. Each fund appeared to have its own investment philosophy and its own separate life. Autonomy here was both rigorous science and high art.

Another important clue surfaced in relation to product development. New-product development was a much-prized skill fueled by personal initiative that hinged on three interdependent capacities:

- Creativity, an inherent ability to challenge assumptions and convention and to identify *investor patterns of behavior* that could be exploited.

- A wholehearted willingness to embrace risk as a basic part of effective "R&D."

- A curious sort of "arms-length intimacy" with customers that was the result of blending formal observations, such as market research, with the personal, intimate observations of managers and employees about what customers really want and need. Arms-length intimacy was very much a part of how the company expressed itself.

How Fidelity's marketing managers segmented and approached customers was another useful source of information about what made the company tick. When it came to customer selection, these executives sought out and catered to the more sophisticated, experienced investor. These were clearly (and not surprisingly) Fidelity's best prospects. They had the money and the appetite. There was more to it than that, however. What emerged during my analysis of its segmentation was Fidelity's innate regard for customer knowledge and self-governance—an enduring respect for investor intelligence and privacy that mirrored how the company regarded itself.

This dynamic was even more clearly evident with corporate clients. On that level, Fidelity managers actively pursued relationships with well-established companies that were guided by very smart managers who could keep up with Fidelity executives. There was little doubt that intelligence and assertiveness in decision making were valued customer attributes. What this translated into was a shared ability to discuss ideas and investment options that reinforced brainpower on both sides of the relationship. Simply put, smart people wanted to deal with other smart people.

One of the most telling clues to Fidelity's identity was how the enterprise looked at productivity among its employees. In the course of numerous interviews, it quickly became clear that Fidelity shied away from standard measures of productivity that merely quantify the output of products or services. Fidelity was much more focused on—if not obsessed with—human achievement. Employee excitement and involvement in new projects such as fund development and customer service improvements (for example, telephone training aimed at turning transactions into relationships) were the real barometers of achievement. Encouraging people to do what they did best was a widely acknowledged means of value creation. Even having fun was a highly prized goal. It was evidence that employees were "cooking," "gassed-up," using their natural-born talents at full throttle.

Even though I was investigating how the company operated at that moment, I was equally interested in going back through the corporate archives, for I knew that the history of the institution would yield its own special insights. Among the stories about the Johnson family, Fidelity's founders, I came upon two pieces of information that were especially compelling. The first revolved around what one of the family members perceived as the role of the stock market itself. In the 1940s, Edward Johnson II regarded the market as *the ultimate arbiter of personal initiative and capability.* I was struck by the grandeur implied by this perception. It wasn't just about making money; Johnson's definition lent human capacities to the market itself. He conceived of it as both judge and jury on the economic potential of people's basic entrepreneurial instincts combined with their God-given talents.

The second important discovery involved a more recent event. In the 1970s, Edward Johnson III made Fidelity one of the first major mutual fund companies to go right to the customer via direct-response marketing. At the time, this was a bold and innovative act of populism. Fidelity's leaders were saying that investments weren't just the province of the select few; investing was a *right* that all enjoyed. Johnson's vision set the stage for reshaping the entire mutual funds industry and, by extension, the world of investments.

My search eventually led me back to the time I had spent in the small, clinical chart room and in Ned Johnson's elegant office. How was it, I thought, that this organization could so easily embrace these two equally important, yet diametrically opposed, spaces? What captured my attention wasn't just the physical contrast; I was intrigued by what I sensed was the interdependence of these two dramatically different environments.

Putting It All Together

All the pieces of the puzzle called Fidelity were at hand. It was now a matter of adding up the evidence. It was time to look at Fidelity much as I might look at any person—any leader—in an attempt to identify and articulate what made him or her unique.

I knew more clearly than ever that what I was doing wasn't about positioning in the conventional sense at all. It was about revealing the *living being*, Fidelity, to those executives responsible for guiding the institution, as well as to the institution itself—with all the attendant implications for strategy, organization, product and service development, and reward and recognition.

The "proof" that I had captured Fidelity's uniqueness would be found in whether my definition of Fidelity's identity answered the pivotal questions contained within Erik Erikson's psychological framework. If that proof existed, then Johnson and Bodman would find themselves standing atop the most powerful platform possible—a platform supported by the three pillars of identity: efficiency, integrity, and endurance.

Would knowing its identity allow Fidelity—its management along with the broader employee population—to trust itself and its actions even more than it already did? Would this knowledge of identity adequately reinforce Fidelity's autonomy as an individual? Would it shed light on the source of Fidelity's phenomenal sense of initiative? Would knowing the firm's identity reveal a central competence that subsumed all others? Would it explain the organization's focus on human achievement as opposed to mere productivity? Finally, would identity—once acknowledged and embraced—help foster pervasive acceptance of "who Fidelity truly is," internally and externally?

An added level of pressure emerged late one evening after a conversation with Rab Bertelsen, one of Fidelity's marketing executives and a primary contact. Rab was convinced that Fidelity was indeed unique. He also knew that any successful institutional strategy would require building on that knowledge. But he was concerned that it might just be too hard to put Fidelity's identity into words. I assured him of two things. First, I emphasized that Fidelity, like all organizations and individuals, contains its own identity—it is simply a fact of life. Second, I reminded him that the process we had been through together was as much about reconstruction—synthesis—as about the analytical process of deconstruction. In the end, the words we needed to make Fidelity's identity clear would be there.

Walking back to the hotel, I retraced my diagnostic steps, asking myself questions for which I had no quick answer. On the surface, Fidelity seemed to be a loose confederation of highly successful entrepreneurs, each pursuing his or her own agenda. But why this overt obsession with operating independence and being one's own boss? Why did so many managers bristle at the idea of authority beyond their domain? Why such vigorous denial of the institution in any form other than name and various administrative functions, such as legal and human resources services? This autonomy had assumed ritual proportions, and I needed to know where it came from.

As I entered my hotel room, an image came to me of DaVinci's drawing of the human form contained within a circle and presented in its two rotations. DaVinci had isolated the individual, celebrating at once his uniqueness and completeness. As I stared at that drawing in my mind, I realized that it was the perfect metaphor for understanding Fidelity's true identity: *This being named Fidelity was driven by the need to celebrate individualism.*

The company's fierce independence and high regard for self-governance—among managers and employees as well as among Fidelity's customers—were chief characteristics that underpinned this need to celebrate individualism. The widely held assumption that autonomous operations were the be all and end all of value creation was false. Operating autonomy was the effect, not the cause. A larger force at work—a life force—was responsible for the fundamental ways in which the enterprise behaved. I realized that each person, fund, department, and division was in fact a manifestation of the very corporate identity that so many people had denied. Management needed to know this. Johnson and Bodman needed to understand that although autonomy was a vital operating philosophy, it had its limits and belonged in its place on a much larger canvas. Fidelity's leaders needed to ensure that operating autonomy ultimately came back to enhance loyalty to the institution, not just to various funds.

An all-consuming drive to celebrate individualism was the essential DNA of the organization. The life-giving chemistry of this corporate being could be explained in terms of a central principle: *The interests of the individual are paramount; all values, rights, and duties originate in individuals; political and economic independence are sacred; and individual initiative, action, and interests are the wellspring of value creation.*

This insight into Fidelity led me quickly back to asking, and answering, the questions inherent in Erikson's definition of identity. *Yes*, I thought, Fidelity could trust itself, its actions, and its motives as a result of its passion for individualism. *Yes*, Fidelity's autonomy in the world around it was secured by this drive. *Yes*, without a doubt, the organization's initiative and towering ambition could be understood by its need to celebrate individualism. *Yes*, this passion stood as Fidelity's center of gravity in terms of competence. *Yes*, the need to celebrate individualism clearly explained why human achievement, not simply productivity, was the focus of the organization.

I finally saw that to understand Fidelity's identity was to understand how the enterprise created value in the deepest sense. If its identity could meet all of these criteria, then it was virtually impossible for Fidelity *not* to create value. It was no wonder that Fidelity had attained leadership in the expanding world of mutual funds.

In that moment, I glimpsed a vital truth about how things in business really worked. I felt as though a nagging mystery had just been solved and that, in turn, a door had opened and I had stepped through. I was struck by the power of identity to influence success and failure, but above all, I was taken by the immense similarities between human beings and organizations.

As I considered Fidelity, DaVinci's drawing of the human form fused in my mind with the organization itself. I saw more clearly than ever that the dynamics of Fidelity and the dynamics of the human being were a mirror image of each other. The physical, mental, and emotional capacities that defined individuality in the one did so in the other as well. Fidelity was an early, unforgettable example. I would spend the next decade testing, refining, and building on this discovery and its implications for leadership.

FROM INDIVIDUALITY TO DIFFERENTIATION

What I was about to ask Fidelity's management to do was to rethink, refine, and realign, in accordance with identity, every facet of how the enterprise conducted itself in the world around it. I was suggesting that Johnson, Bodman, and others put aside their tacit assumptions about management's ability to "control" and simply set direction for the organization. I was asking that these successful senior executives take stock of the inherent identity of their enterprise and then act to deepen and enrich this identity in the name of value creation.

For me, the logic of doing so was self-evident. Like any human being, this unique corporate entity had its own way of seeing things and behaving in relation to others. Its identity was a gyroscope that was fully capable of setting the organization on a productive course in its environment. Management's job was to let it do so.

Of course, the company's identity had been there all along. Identity is ever-present. Fidelity's need to celebrate individualism had been part of the enterprise for as long as it had been in existence. The problem, as far as I could tell, was that no one within Fidelity was aware that this identity existed, let alone what it was. As a result, executives were not in a position to steer the company in ways that would let it capitalize fully on its value-creating potential.

As I considered the possible changes that management faced, I recalled my original task. I was retained to help spark customer loyalty to the institution, which entailed answering the basic question *"Loyalty to what?"* The answer was now clear: *Loyalty to an institution that was unique in its celebration of the individual.*

It was only after I felt I had cracked the code, however, that the way to pursue Johnson's stated goal—achieving greater customer loyalty to the institution—became apparent: Do everything possible to align identity with what the market wanted. Because of growing demand for personalized customer service, Fidelity executives at all levels would need to learn how to "sell" Fidelity's identity as though it were a product in its own right. In simple terms, celebrate in every way possible the individuality of the customer. Seize this ready-made opportunity for management to capitalize on the institution's birthright.

It was now March 1985. I had been working on the case for nearly four months and was scheduled to give my initial presentation to a group of managers in April. The first presentation was to Rab Bertelsen and a few other marketing executives who had sponsored the study. This meeting was a turning point in my professional life. It was a moment I wouldn't soon forget. I was about to present ideas about Fidelity that I knew would put me in a potentially risky position with Rab, for I wasn't at all sure how he and his colleagues would react.

Everything in my report hinged on "Clarifying the Distinctiveness of Fidelity to Achieve Competitive Advantage," the title of the first section of the document. On the surface, this was a reasonable and unsurprising "deliverable" for a positioning assignment. It was within this section, however, that I presented the two thoughts that, combined, were indeed radical: that Fidelity was *alive,* a self-directing being in its own right, and that this unique individual called Fidelity could be known through its *identity*, which formed through the convergence of its particular mental, physical, and emotional capacities.

What now appeared so logical and self-evident—even simple—had been utterly obscure only four months earlier. I had laid bare the human capacities of the organization in order to understand the basic chemistry that had impelled it to a position of leadership in the world of financial services.

My central conclusion—that Fidelity was driven by the need to celebrate individualism—elicited quiet stares from Rab and his associates. I continued, presenting the supporting evidence and making all the necessary connections to how Fidelity should "position" itself to build customer loyalty to the institution. The members of the group began to ask probing questions about identity and what it meant in relation to how Fidelity behaved internally as well as externally. The ideas began to sink in. People were making connections between Fidelity's identity and how the organization went about winning customers and making money.

That night, when Rab and I were walking to dinner, he recalled his initial concern: that I would either come up empty-handed or simply restate the obvious about Fidelity's superior financial services know-how, albeit perhaps in more distinctive ways. As I listened, I took pleasure in seeing that Rab "got it." He was clearly moved by my conclusion about Fidelity's identity. It had struck a chord in him, and his excitement was apparent.

I saw in Rab at that moment a man who had long wanted to believe that his company was in some way alive and unique but who, until that day, had been either unsure of the fact or unwilling to admit it. I believe the results of the study were personally liberating for Rab, confirming his implicit belief in the life of the enterprise.

Among the many managers I got to know, Rab stood out. With the new knowledge he had just gained, Rab's capacity for leadership grew dramatically; he understood what direction Fidelity was taking. Rab possessed an unusual combination of human insight and business pragmatism, and he took it upon himself to champion the power of identity. Over the next few weeks, he drafted a comprehensive plan for implementation. It almost seemed easy. On the strength of his now-explicit understanding of Fidelity's identity, Rab knew instinctively how to proceed.

Most of Rab's proposed changes focused on strengthening Fidelity's front-line relationships with customers. In an effort to operationalize identity, he homed in on changes that linked organization and customer interaction:

- Designing an employee training program to ensure a "one-Fidelity" approach that emphasized individualism so that all employees would understand the meaning of Fidelity and realize that their "job" was essentially to reinforce this organizing principle.

- Recalibrating all customer service hiring criteria in order to identify and recruit people who would understand the tenets of individualism and apply them to all aspects of customer relationships.

- Instituting customer relations awards for outstanding service reps whose actions clearly demonstrated Fidelity's commitment to the individual.

- Turning Fidelity's investor centers into full-service, storefront investment operations, with knowledgeable staff, comprehensive touch-screen computers, and educational programs for first-time as well as veteran investors. Doing so made the company much more accessible to individuals. (For Fidelity, retailing was a natural environment for expressing its identity; the strategy was signally consistent with "who Fidelity was.")

- Conducting research to find out how many customers had personal computers and modems and then developing an on-line database that would provide daily fund N.A.V.s (net asset values) and other fund information, all of which, in turn, would strenghten the bond between the investor and the institution.

Rab thus crafted an action plan that reached into the entire marketing organization of Fidelity and then some. Seventeen different operations were engaged, from the telephone service, wire room, and correspondence department, to retail, wholesale, pension, and institutional marketing, to the legal and human resource functions. He had charted the path for Fidelity to distinguish itself and, in doing so, connect with its investors in ways that would build directly on Fidelity's unique ability to deal with customers "individual to individual."

I had provided management with the foundation it needed for building loyalty to the institution. Customers, employees, and others whose lives and livelihoods were affected by Fidelity would benefit from aligning themselves with an organization that, above all else, needed to celebrate their individuality in every way possible. Many of the actions proposed by Rab affected day-to-day operations. These initiatives rapidly began to ensure that Fidelity's passion for individualism would become the bridge between the institution and its customers.

For management, as for the rest of the company, knowing the institution as a unique entity was the key to being understood by others in ways that were impossible for any competitor to replicate. For Johnson and Bodman, Fidelity's identity was the ultimate source of differentiation. Others might claim a similar commitment, say, to meeting customer's "individual needs," but no others had it in their blood. None lived it as a world view. No competitor, however large, strong, or aggressive, could "out-Fidelity" Fidelity. The company's pervasive *commitment to individualism* was, and remains, the cornerstone of its market leadership—an iron defense, impenetrable by would-be predators.

The Law of Individuality contains the answer to one of the most vital and vexing questions facing all companies: *What business are we in?* In Fidelity's case, is the company in the mutual funds business? The financial services business? The answer is both—and neither. To be sure, Fidelity's business is predicated on its deep expertise in financial services, generally, and on its extraordinary capacity for developing, selling, and managing mutual funds, specifically. But all of these skills, products, and services are vehicles through which Fidelity as a whole engages its customers. *Fidelity Investments is in the business of celebrating individualism.* That is how the institution creates value. Everything else—its funds, its discount brokerage services, its pension and institutional marketing, its investor centers, *everything*—is a cog in the wheel of value creation.

Despite how it can help leaders get to the bottom of what makes their companies different, the Law of Individuality is often challenged by a *paradox of differentiation* that gets in the way of living by this law. As much as managers yearn for their organizations to be different in the eyes of customers, employees, investors, and other constituencies, they hesitate to get to the heart of knowing their companies' true identities, which is where meaningful distinction lies.

The "disconnect" between what managers want and what they are willing to do to get it is the result of two myths that have found their way into business life. The first myth is that the ways in which companies and people operate are vastly different. Nothing could be further from the truth. Companies are, in fact, the nearly perfect, organizational extrapolation of a human being, exhibiting (as I noted earlier) distinct physical, cognitive, and emotional characteristics. Contrary to this myth, managers must understand that their organizations are alive and have distinctive characteristics all their own.

The second myth many managers subscribe to is that their organizations have already fallen prey to homogenization—the result of continuous selection and de-selection in recruiting, hiring, and firing. But the opposite it true. What actually happens through the screening process is profound individuation. The filtering process relentlessly *refines* and *deepens* the unique identity of the organization by attracting and holding people who are inherently in sync with it.

What *does* occur in the name of differentiation is usually one of two things. The first is that managers tend to differentiate their company on the basis of products and services, culture and economics. It is no surprise that this happens. Products and services are easy to see and know: "The most dependable washers and dryers" or "A full-choice provider of personal financial services." Cultural values can be defined and articulated via *behaviors* that are fairly easy to document.

"We're the quality leaders." "Service is us." Economic exigencies are pervasive and, because of their direct effect on business performance, become comfort zones for differentiation (low-cost provider equals "everyday low prices").

The second thing that happens in the name of differentiation is that companies, through their own efforts or in collaboration with advertising agencies or other marketing services firms, *manufacture* identities that may have little basis in reality. Or they try to do so, only to alter these identities when people—customers, investors, recruits, and others—don't respond as they had hoped. Well-intentioned managers often know that they are fooling themselves (and by extension others), or they may have come to believe that true distinctiveness just isn't possible.

The inescapable fact is, however, that differentiation in any form other than differentiation based on identity isn't sustainable. This is because it lacks roots, and without roots, it is destined to collapse under pressure—pressure from technological innovation, pressure from lower-cost providers, pressure from competitors' successful new-product developments, and so on. By contrast, identity supplies these roots. It affirms the individuality of organizations, making that individuality a reliable framework for action. On the strength of identity, differentiation achieves integrity and can be trusted.

To come to terms with the Law of Individuality is to grasp the true nature and purpose of the enterprise. Armed with this knowledge, leaders are in the strongest possible position to lead. Strategy and change initiatives, explained within the context of identity, become understandable—and far more palatable—to everyone involved. Why? Because the leader's direction isn't the product of a management committee. It flows instead from the unique capacities of the entire enterprise. Everyone is part of it. Everyone can find themselves in it. It has deep credibility. It has roots.

One of the overarching ways in which acknowledging, affirming, and operationalizing identity benefits leadership is that it turbo-boosts a company's ability to create value at every level. It does this by getting everyone to "serve" the identity of the enterprise, while simultaneously drawing on the unique skills, creativity, and energy of those involved. As a result, the organization is tuned to pursue the three key features of identity: grand efficiency, integrity, and endurance. Because they were governed by Rab's understanding of the organization's identity, Rab Bertelsen's actions at Fidelity contained their own natural efficiency and integrity. These two vital qualities, in turn, dramatically increase Fidelity's chances of enduring over time.

No doubt, systems have to be in place to organize and prioritize activities and monitor progress. But the "pull" of identity creates its own system of checks and balances that people can apply across the business, assuming that they are aware of what the company's identity is in the first place. From this perspective, to crack the code on identity is to crack the code on leadership.

For individuals and companies alike, the power generated once identity is known bestows many benefits, including impenetrable armor against one's detractors. For individuals and companies alike, the power of understanding one's identity also becomes a magnet for attracting friends, partners, and (in the case of businesses) customers, employees, and investors.

Identity is the bedrock of differentiation. For people who want to lead others, it is the wellspring of personal development and growth—an important prerequisite of leadership. For corporate leaders hell-bent on value creation, identity is the source—the only conceivable source—of sustainable competitive advantage.

No one can take away your birthright.

3 THE LAW OF CONSTANCY

IDENTITY IS FIXED, TRANSCENDING TIME AND PLACE, WHILE ITS MANIFESTATIONS ARE CONSTANTLY CHANGING.

*I am alive, I am unique, **and I am immutable,
even as I grow and evolve.***
*To truly live, however, I must express myself fully,
and in this regard, have much to give.*
*But to do so, I need others, and am most productive
with those who need me in return.*
*To establish these relationships, I must first be
recognized for who I am,
and it follows then that*
I will receive in accordance with what I give.

In the past decade, no issue has occupied the business leader more than change—specifically, the need for change and how to achieve it. Leaders such as Jack Welch of General Electric and Percy Barnevik of Asea Brown Boveri are looked upon as change masters. They've made change part of the everyday fabric of the organizations they lead. Yet amid all the change they have inspired, these leaders have managed to maintain a sense of constancy about who the organization is and what it stands for. For all the change that goes on at GE, the company still "brings good things to life"—a popular expression of its underlying identity.

One of the best-known and most successful change stories in recent years belongs to Xerox under the leadership of CEO Paul Allaire. The story of change at Xerox is about transforming the organization from a copier company to the "document" company, and significant change was measured in terms of improved return on assets, increased market share and the boosting of employee morale. It wasn't the copying equipment that was Xerox's franchise; it was everything that went through that equipment.

Despite the massive shifts in investment priorities, personnel, and culture that Allaire orchestrated, change in the company was in many ways no change at all. Xerox was born to be a document company. It was its birthright. Paul Allaire's genius was in recognizing this fact—and then letting Xerox be Xerox. It is the nature of constancy that some things just do not change, no matter how different they may seem.

The changes I have experienced, and continue to experience as I grow, I now know are as much illusion as real. My life seems to have moved in a series of dynamic amplitudes, from a childhood in which I depended on art and music for recognition from others, to teenage years dedicated to experimenting with individual sports such as Tae kwon do and swimming, to a series of tentative, early career moves, to the unparalleled joy I found at Anspach Grossman Portugal, and on and on.

In the course of these years, I have embraced, seemingly abandoned, and finally reaffirmed, my love for things creative—for creativity itself. The primitive sculptures of bears I shaped when I was eight, the rough-hewn still-lifes I painted when I was fourteen, the essays I crafted when I was twenty, the market research I conducted when I was twenty-eight, and the discoveries I made about Fidelity's identity when I was thirty-four are all perfectly consistent with who I am now, at forty-nine, and with who I will be for the rest of my life.

It is comforting to know that change doesn't necessarily mean abandoning all things. And sometimes what we see as change isn't change at all; it is another way of expressing who we are. The Law of Constancy, the third Law of Identity, highlights the limits of change, imposing a discipline on us all: *Not to lose sight of the immutable, unique characteristics that allow each of us to create value in our world.* In reminding us that identity is "fixed," irrespective of time and place, this law compels us to take stock of how well we're doing in expressing and applying our identity at any given moment.

How is my unrelenting passion for things creative being exercised? Is the "rabbi" within me able to confer with clients on things that make a difference in their particular organizations and in their lives? Is my "architect" testing his craft by forging a picture of the corporation—say, Fidelity—as it might be were it to organize itself around, and operate in accordance with, its need to celebrate individualism? The discipline imposed by the Law of Constancy is the mandate to exercise interpretation within a sea of changes occurring around us.

Few managers run their businesses according to the Law of Constancy, because they simply do not realize that it exists, as the law of gravity. Today, wholesale change is often seen as the path to salvation where nothing seems to be sacred. But that is wrong. *Identity* is sacred. To ignore this third Law of Identity is to invite failure. Short of the total disassembling of a company—of the corporate being—identity will not be denied.

There are, however, a number of companies across diverse industries whose history and longevity suggest that they do operate in accordance with the Law of Constancy, even if they do so unwittingly. Caterpillar, General Electric, Matsushita, Coca-Cola, Boeing, Maytag, Arthur Andersen, McKinsey & Co., Goldman Sachs, even Fidelity and Alcoa—all fit this mold. In many ways, they are larger than life. Often they are "most admired" by their peers. They are special. They are the leaders in their fields.

Korn/Ferry International is one organization that abides instinctively by the third Law of Identity. In the field of executive search, Korn/Ferry has been the largest in terms of revenues, and its global reach is unmatched. But it is in other ways that the success of this industry leader comes to light, revealing along the way how the Law of Constancy guided its growth and evolution.

KORN/FERRY INTERNATIONAL

Century City—The Introduction

My meeting with Michael Boxberger, then Korn/Ferry's CEO, took place in a small, undistinguished conference room well inside the firm's cluster of offices in Century City, California. Aside from a collection of "corporate" paintings—art without passion—that covered the walls, there was nothing to distract one from the business at hand.

Korn/Ferry's partners had come to realize that they needed to differentiate the firm as part of their efforts to change. They were feeling the pressure of competition from the likes of Heidrick & Struggles, Egon Zehnder International, and others.

Michael was deliberate and thoughtful, nearly rehearsed in his choice of words and war stories about the economic benefits of differentiating the firm and about its personal impact on partners in terms of both their sense of commitment to the organization and their compensation.

In preparing for this meeting, I had come across a survey, published in *Executive Recruiter News* just a month before, of the forty largest retained search firms in the United States. I had brought the survey with me and decided to put it on the table as a centerpiece for discussion. As I did, I remarked to Michael that although Korn/Ferry certainly ranked number one in U.S. revenues—$104,000,000 in 1995—the firm's revenues-per-professional ratio put it well down the list. SpencerStuart and boutiques such as McCann Choi & Associates took the lead on that measure.

Michael's studied calm gave way to a spontaneous diatribe on the misleading nature of this particular survey result. In his view, this ratio was a one-dimensional barometer of success that diverted attention from the underlying strength of Korn/Ferry as measured by its distinctive strategy, structure, and culture. This moment, and the moments that immediately followed, were the first substantive clues I would collect about the true identity of Korn/Ferry International.

Among other things, Michael explained in painstaking detail the apparently arbitrary distinction between "professionals" and "partners" that skewed the numbers. He had, as he indicated, fought this battle before, trying to get outsiders to understand what was, in his and his partners' minds, a crucial difference that was central to understanding what it meant to be Korn/Ferry.

In nearly every professional services firm, revenues per professional, or partner, is a key success measure that is laden with meaning, not only in terms of implied profitability, growth, and personal wealth, but also at a more visceral level: client recognition and overall perceived value. I sensed that Michael's frustration ran deeper than annoyance at the limited insight offered up by this statistic.

The survey, dense with numbers, was printed in black and white on one side of a single piece of paper whose edges had become crumpled and gray from my repeated readings. Visually speaking, it was an entirely forgettable document. But, by omission, the story it told was actually vibrant with color, full of nuance, and bathed in the light and shadows of an organization whose value was impossible to quantify in such simplistic terms.

Korn/Ferry was richer, more complicated, and more dynamic than I had at first surmised. Once its identity became clear to me, I would realized how Korn/Ferry had in fact made constancy its journey-mate since its inception, nearly thirty years earlier. I would also understand why Michael Boxberger had so passionately rejected the revenues-per-professional ratio as a meaningful gauge of Korn/Ferry's worth: It just wasn't relevant to how the organization created value.

Finding the Brand

Marketing and branding are two business disciplines that professional services firms generally have been slow to embrace. Possibly this is because both areas have been largely associated with consumer products. Or it may be that the traditional professional services' focus on individual contribution prevented people from seeing the whole of the organization as greater than the sum of its parts—a prerequisite to defining and managing any corporate brand.

It was clear from the outset of my engagement with Korn/Ferry that a majority of partners around the world—in particular, managing partners—had gotten over any doubts about the need to come to terms with the brand. Their desire to build global relationships with leading corporations had galvanized people's interest in understanding what it meant to be Korn/Ferry International and, by extension, how "the brand" could be translated to meet multinational, regional, or local needs.

Clarifying the brand—as I described it to Korn/Ferry, *the promise the company makes to its stakeholders*—had become a management priority. My job was to identify and align Korn/Ferry's identity characteristics in a way that would help achieve this goal, allowing the organization to move smoothly along its already-established path of institutional leadership. As I saw it, I didn't need to help my client define its brand; I needed to help them *find it*.

No matter how it was phrased, I knew one thing for certain: Clarifying what it meant to be Korn/Ferry required dealing with the firm as a whole. Individuals would now have to take a back seat and let the institution take its turn as the star. I realized that shifting the focus in this way, and in virtually everything the firm did, would be very tough for a professional services business that, like others in its field, had traditionally been driven by star consultants and by compensation plans designed to reward individual performance above all other things.

The search business had managed to come late to the differentiation party. By now, companies in other sectors—accounting, investment banking, and various consulting firms, for instance—had already succeeded in making marketing and brand development part of their on-going management process. Shining examples in this area include Goldman Sachs, Andersen Consulting, and McKinsey & Company.

By the time I began working with Korn/Ferry, it was clear, both through quantitative surveys and anecdotally, that no executive search organization had successfully differentiated itself. The "plain vanilla" label had been assigned to virtually all firms by corporate managers around the world.

How, I wondered, had this vital segment of the professional services industry managed to keep itself so perfectly undistinguished, one firm from the next? As a first step in understanding how this had come about, I pored over the literature and websites of major organizations, making lists of the key words and terms that each firm used to describe itself. I wanted to see what, if any, themes emerged.

I quickly identified eighteen attributes cited as points of differentiation among Korn/Ferry and its four principal competitors, Heidrick & Struggles, SpencerStuart, Russell Reynolds, and Egon Zehnder. What I found was that, of these eighteen attributes, nine points that were meant to be distinguishing were essentially *identical* among all of these firms. These attributes included global reach, local presence, industry-specific expertise, partnership approach, quality, and partner experience.

In making similar claims, these five dominant firms had unwittingly contributed to the market's perception that they were "all the same." It was no wonder, I thought, that clients had turned to individual partners rather than to the organizations all these years; they had had no choice since institutional identities were all but buried.

It is axiomatic in the world of branding that no one person, however powerful or well known, is more powerful than the organization he or she created. Why is this? Because of two simple facts. The first is that the organization, given the hundreds or thousands of people in it, necessarily embodies greater knowledge than its founder, and it is this knowledge that leads to innovations for customers over time, in turn deepening both the real and the perceived value of the brand.

The second fact is self-evident: People ultimately die. Organizations, properly managed, have the potential to live forever.

Breaking out of the pack presented a major challenge for Korn/ Ferry, and I knew that finding the organization's brand also meant finding a path from founder identity, most recently that of Richard Ferry, to institutional identity, orchestrated at the time by Michael Boxberger and his team. Such transitions, of course, are natural passages for all companies, but they take on greater significance in the context of identity-based management, and they assume acute importance in light of the Law of Constancy.

In the previous fifteen years, I had worked with a number of organizations, private as well as public, where either the founder or a member of the founding family was still in a position of leadership. What had I learned from these experiences that I could apply now to Korn/Ferry? Exactly what steps would be called for to ensure that this leadership transition served the institution's larger brand development needs? The answers—those "steps"—were quickly forthcoming. Continuing the transition from Richard Ferry to "Korn/Ferry" would require

- Identifying and codifying the vital characteristics the founder had instilled in the beginning.

- At the same time, allowing that individual himself to recede, but not so much as to be lost as the firm grew and evolved.

- Not allowing new managers to devise strategy that turned a blind eye to the past, especially to identity-based strengths that link the past to the future.

- Encouraging growth that would add to and refresh the vision of the founder.

All in, what I had learned was that leadership transitions—in this case, Korn/Ferry's—meant allowing the corporate being itself to "take over" and move ahead under its own steam. Korn/Ferry's transition required a bridge that belonged to neither management generation but would, rather, be owned by future generations.

Seven Enduring Qualities

I had soon identified seven dominant characteristics of Korn/Ferry. Each could be traced historically—often back to the company's roots nearly three decades earlier—and each told a part of the story about the unique nature of this institutional being.

The first characteristic was Korn/Ferry's *professionalism*—more specifically, the company's unrelenting drive to "professionalize" the search business. One of the most telling pieces of evidence about the firm was a speech that Richard Ferry had delivered to The Newcomen Society in 1994. This speech was rich in information from which I was able to learn much and draw numerous implications. Korn/Ferry's passion for bringing better business practices and standards to search was part and parcel of Richard Ferry's and Lester Korn's founding philosophy. It was never not there.

Both men were determined to make executive search a true management discipline—a respected and valued profession. I noted that at one point in his speech, Ferry termed executive search "a way of life." It was a statement of his conviction about how the search profession influenced the way clients and consultants alike perceived the world and the problems and challenges it held. Executive search was more than just a business.

This idea was expanded on through another source: a book written by John Byrne, a senior writer for *Business Week*. In *The Headhunters*, Byrne wrote, "Korn/Ferry has revolutionized and institutionalized the business, and has helped transform the way executives switch jobs." When I read this, I recalled what the notion of institution is all about. An "institution" is an organization that has clear connections with the culture outside of itself, with society at large. How, exactly, had Korn/Ferry made this connection?

Another central characteristic of the firm was its *business problem-solving approach* to building client relationships. In his Newcomen speech, Richard Ferry noted the firm's "obsession with understanding clients." He had a need to understand what made the company and its managers special. Ferry put a premium on his clients' uniqueness as a prerequisite to meeting their search needs.

Korn/Ferry also had a strong track record of establishing new products and practice. These included assistance in the areas of executive compensation and organizational development, management succession planning, and consulting on team building and leadership effectiveness. In yet another aspect of its problem-solving orientation, Korn/Ferry was one of the first consultancies to invest in specialization around industries, among them financial services, health care, technology, and manufacturing.

Size was a third distinguishing characteristic of the enterprise. It was one of those attributes that had become a rallying cry for the firm's partners. Bigness meant something to Korn/Ferry. In 1989 the firm was the first to exceed $100 million in revenues. In 1994 that number grew to over $150 million. Korn/Ferry boasted of its 400 professionals and 1800 client organizations. Today, the firm has placed over 70,000 managers worldwide. A majority of the partners I spoke with believed that *size* was a crucial point of differentiation.

Close on the heels of size, *global reach* surfaced as one of the most powerful aspects of the firm. Once again, the numbers told their own story. Korn/Ferry was the first truly global firm, with forty-eight offices in twenty-six countries, and more than half its professionals worked outside the United States. As I listened to partners and clients and reviewed company literature, it became clear that relentless expansion into all corners of the world was a defining feature of Korn/Ferry. The firm had merged with Carré/Orban, the largest organization in Europe, in 1993. It had opened offices in Scandinavia and Luxembourg and, more recently, in Moscow and St. Petersburg, Mexico City, Caracas, Bogota, and Buenos Aires. What I found particularly visionary, however, was that the founders had opened an office in Tokyo in 1973—years before Japan emerged as an economic superpower. Today, the firm also has a presence in Bangkok, Singapore, Hong Kong, and Kuala Lumpur.

The sheer physical achievements of the organization were impressive. I could feel the momentum—and the expectations—that size and reach, together, had created. There was a sense of manifest destiny about the company that fueled its passion for growth. At that moment, a seemingly incidental thought crossed my mind. In his speech to The

Newcomen Society, Richard Ferry had recalled how he and Lester Korn foresaw a global economy and decided, then and there, to name their firm Korn/Ferry International.

Korn/Ferry's *governance structure* also emerged as a distinguishing feature. Since its inception, the company's aim had been to operate as one firm; Ferry had spoken in his Newcomen Society address of a diverse work force unified by a shared vision and values. What I read into this was his desire to maintain the whole at all costs, no matter how large it became. This goal was served as well by ensuring that all Korn/Ferry offices were run by full-fledged partners: no associates, no franchises, no loose affiliations. No one was going to undermine the integrity of this corporate being.

The sixth defining characteristic of Korn/Ferry was its passion for *new knowledge*—to create it and to share it, internally and externally. Just as the firm had invested significantly in people, offices, and technology, it had also invested heavily in research. The focus of this research, not surprisingly, was on important management and corporate governance issues. Korn/Ferry's leaders also invested in public relations. Why? To help educate the media, and then business, about Korn/Ferry and executive search in general: how it worked, how it added value, what standards and service the client should expect.

The firm's pursuit of new knowledge extended to its decision to put resources behind research in cooperation with leading universities. In 1973, for example, Korn/Ferry sponsored the first roundtable on corporate governance in conjunction with the University of Pennsylvania. Since then, the firm has undertaken an annual Board of Directors study to measure the pulse of corporate America through board trends; the program continues to this day. The University of Pennsylvania, Columbia, Yale, USC, and UCLA had all become part of what I saw as a loosely organized research federation that linked the organization to the outside world. Yes, these research efforts were good for business, but in and of themselves, they also yielded new and timely knowledge, ranging from the changing profiles of leaders to in-depth studies of executive women in the workplace.

Korn/Ferry was a classic learning organization. It thrived—commercially and intellectually—on new knowledge. As I considered this dimension of the company, I realized that I hadn't gone quite far enough. Korn/Ferry was more than a learning organization; it was also a *teaching* organization. Its place on the map of industry leadership was long ago assured, born of its particular connection to society and culture through education.

The seventh characteristic I identified was Korn/Ferry's bias toward *multilevel, multifunctional searches*. Most search firms focused on, and aggressively promoted, their high-level placements: CEOs, presidents, chief financial officers, and other top-management jobs. This is glamorous work: high fees, high income, high stakes. Without a doubt, Korn/Ferry had its share of this high-end business. But the firm's search orientation—its particular approach to helping clients shape the management infrastructure of their organizations—took its partners notably deeper into the companies it served. Key middle manager and director-level posts across functions were also important venues for Korn/Ferry. Human resources, manufacturing, finance, communications, sales and marketing—along with top management and boards—were all familiar territory for the organization.

One of the ways the firm expressed its bias toward breadth and depth was through *Korn/Ferry Selection*, its advertised search service across Europe, Latin America, and Asia/Pacific. The notion of broad-based advertising to the masses ran against the grain of exclusivity that marked traditional retained search. But it did extend the firm's reach and influence well into the mid-level job community in key markets around the world.

Korn/Ferry's commitment to multilevel, multifunctional searches was at once a blessing and a curse. It was a blessing in that it expanded the firm's revenue base and its influence with its clients. But it was also a curse in that Korn/Ferry was often unfairly characterized by competitors as largely focused on "mid-level," rather than senior, management search. In the course of my interviews, this subject elicited strong defensive reactions on the part of Korn/Ferry partners. Most regarded the firm's multilevel orientation as a strength misunderstood by those who just "didn't get it."

During the time I worked with Korn/Ferry, I watched as this particular characteristic came to life in a unique and timely way. After much discussion, the partners decided to launch, in association with the *Wall Street Journal*, a new service called *FutureStep*. *FutureStep* was an on-line, career management program that invited people to submit their credentials, which were then reviewed, categorized, and tracked by Korn/Ferry professionals. The program was clearly aimed at mid-level managers with bright futures. Although some partners and outsiders felt this was too popular a medium (read "too downscale") for an exclusive executive search organization, I believed it would prove to be right on target. It was a leading-edge, contemporary expression of Korn/Ferry's bias toward multilevel, multifunctional search. As I saw it, this "new" idea was really vintage Korn/Ferry.

As I considered the history of the firm and its founders' initial passion to professionalize the business, I realized the significance of this seventh dimension. Korn/Ferry's dedication to getting below the surface of client companies—addressing middle manager, director-level, senior management, and board-level needs simultaneously—yielded a far deeper, hands-on understanding of a client company's organizational structure and culture. Not surprisingly, being understood in this way became a source of comfort to senior client executives. They could "trust" Korn/Ferry, and this produced greater interdependence between the concerns.

Had changes occurred during the thirty years since Korn/Ferry was founded? Of course. The firm had succeeded in navigating the course of three decades, each of which posed different challenges. The firm opened its doors as the sixties were coming to an end. It had been the era of the organization man, whose approach to getting to the top was quite linear: one rung of the ladder at a time. Endurance and loyalty were the vital executive values.

The seventies were marked by the hunt for superstar MBAs in their twenties and thirties. These young, ambitious people brought to the work force lots of ideas and energy, but little real-life experience. Then there were the eighties, which Richard Ferry termed the era of "glamorous mega-managers." Premiums on senior executives rose dramatically. Buyout kings reigned, and, as the business press reported, many CEOs lost touch with their own limitations and vulnerabilities. The eighties bowed to what have been the dynamic nineties, as the great bull market led to the most highly compensated group of managers ever, in part, the result of rich stock option plans. At the same time, there has been more willingness on the part of boards of directors to dump ineffective managers and replace them, often quite publicly, with more objective outsiders.

Despite all this change—the management fads and fashions as well as the more substantive, long-lived social, economic, and management trends—I realized just how constant Korn/Ferry had been through it all. The Law of Constancy cautions us to avoid fads, be wary of fashion, take judicious advantage of trends, and cleave resolutely to the identity that outlasts them all. Korn/Ferry had managed to do just that.

What was at the core of this organization that had stayed its course so well over time and had grown and evolved while maintaining its center of gravity? How exactly was it that Korn/Ferry, the institutional being, created value? I knew that value creation held the key to understanding the firm's identity. It is a timeless process that by its very nature adheres to the tenets of the Law of Constancy.

I observed that on the whole, Korn/Ferry partners sought to build some kind of critical mass inside client companies where the firm's impact transcended the individuals they placed. The transactional nature of the search business just didn't adequately describe what made these people tick.

Korn/Ferry's effect on client companies was not only physical, filling offices and the boxes on the organization chart, but also intellectual. Because of Korn/Ferry's propensity to "go broad and deep" within organizations, the firm had a profound effect on the overall knowledge base of a company. And, of course, its effect was human—Korn/Ferry had a significant impact on client culture. The physical, intellectual, and human influence the firm exerted on its clients was striking. Its business *mechanism* was executive search, but its business, I thought, was something else entirely. This organization was aiming to shape the infrastructure of organizations.

Late on a Friday afternoon in January, almost four months after I started my assignment, I was sitting in my office. My desk and credenza were covered with notes from interviews, content analyses of speeches, company literature, and outside research on the industry as a whole that helped me frame the task at hand. The words *depth* and *breadth* kept running through my mind, as did Richard Ferry's passion for his business. As the founder said at the end of his address to The Newcomen Society, "From our inception, Korn/Ferry has been a serious firm . . . serious about establishing search as a true management discipline, about building the international resources to be a great professional firm, about serving clients with integrity, efficiency and commitment. . . . Our mission for the next twenty-five years is to continue this seriousness of purpose. . . ."

Suddenly, it all added up. Korn/Ferry International was, and had always been, driven by *the need to build leadership capital*. The significance of this fact, in terms of differentiating the firm, quickly became clear. From the beginning, this institution knew that to take advantage of their financial, human, and intellectual capital, companies must first build leadership capital—the collective management resources that set all other assets in motion. Korn/Ferry had grasped this cause-and-effect relationship intuitively and had possessed the innate talent to build its franchise around it.

FROM INSIGHT TO ACTION

Building global relationships was not a sure thing. Korn/Ferry faced any number of hurdles as it pursued this strategy. But I believed the firm's chances of clearing these hurdles were good given how it had adhered to the Law of Constancy as a cornerstone of value creation. Why? Because the Law of Constancy, the third Law of Identity, favors those organizations—and those individuals—who build on strengths that are timeless. This is no surprise because the seeds of true leadership—leadership that is earned rather than simply assumed—need time to take root.

Of the many challenges Korn/Ferry faced, taking control of the brand was at the top of the list. Despite its commitment to marketing (on-going investments had been made in pubic relations and client communications), it seemed to me that outsiders, including competitors, had had a greater effect on Korn/Ferry's image than Korn/Ferry itself. For instance, the notion that Korn/Ferry was trying to be all things to all people—reportedly a widely held view among other search organizations—was notably wrong. As more than one partner had told me during the course of my interviews, outsiders simply didn't understand what Korn/Ferry was all about.

Taking control of the brand was a challenge that encompassed all others, bringing me full circle in terms of the original assignment: *Differentiate Korn/Ferry International.* For Korn/Ferry, as for all organizations, the identity of the institution *was* the brand. For thirty years the firm's identity had embodied the unspoken promise Korn/Ferry made to its clients—that the firm would *help them build the leadership capital they required* to leverage all other assets and grow in an ever-changing world.

To take control of the brand meant operationalizing it, not simply communicating it. One opportunity, I realized, would be to differentiate the organization further by designing a special index that quantified the value of leadership capital. The criteria for doing so were many, and the impact of such an index on Korn/Ferry's global relationships promised to be great. Such an index could contain data, both hard and soft, illuminating the overall influence that Korn/Ferry-placed managers had had on the performance of a client organization over time.

A number of yardsticks came to mind: changes in financial performance during a manager's tenure in a certain job; the rate of employee retention, or turnover, during this period; the economic impact of business and product innovations developed and introduced on a manager's watch; the rate of market expansion—local, regional, or global—under that executive's leadership; the overall impact of a manager on the career growth of the people in his or her unit; the relative standing of that manager in the context of overall executive performance reviews.

Each manager would be, in effect, a discrete data point. It was in assessing them in the aggregate—the dozens or hundreds of individuals placed by Korn/Ferry in a particular company—that a Leadership

Capital Index that could be immensely useful to client organizations might evolve.

~

It was December 1997. I had been invited to present my findings and conclusions to Korn/Ferry's executive committee and international advisory board, a group of chief executives from around the world who provided the firm's partners with advice and perspective. I had interviewed many of them in the course of my engagement. The meeting was held in a large, nondescript room at the Four Seasons Hotel in Washington, D.C.

By this time, I had worked on many such assignments. I felt I had come to understand the dynamics of identity—how the life of the corporate being has the power to govern all things and how its individuality is the wellspring of differentiation. Still, I felt especially strongly about this client, about what I had discovered, and about its enormous implications for the company's growth.

Over the next thirty minutes, I went through my presentation. I found myself stepping well into the U-shaped space the tables formed, looking directly and deeply into the eyes of my audience. I spoke, listened, answered questions, and just watched as these men and women considered the subject at hand. At the end of the presentation, nearly everyone in the room applauded. I was caught entirely off guard. It wasn't the polite applause typically offered as a thank-you at the end of a presentation; it was genuine and spontaneous. One of the executive committee members looked at me and said, "You have touched a chord; you understand who we are."

The enthusiasm of many of the partners also bred concerns. One was that competitors might also claim that they built leadership capital. I reassured Boxberger and his associates that although no one can control the actions of others, their anxiety was unfounded. Korn/Ferry owned this turf. Ironically, even the criticisms that had been leveled at the organization—that it was focused on "the middle," that it attempted to be all things to all people—turned out to be evidence of the firm's great strength. So too, I now realized, was Korn/Ferry's deceptively modest ranking, in terms of revenues per professional, that had appeared in the *Executive Recruiter News* survey some six months earlier.

Shortly after this meeting, the partners adopted a new mission for the firm: "to help clients acquire leadership capital—the management asset that sets all others into motion." It was a decision—in fact, a vital moment—that wedded the company's past and present to its future. In embracing this mission, Korn/Ferry had once again observed the Law of Constancy.

Korn/Ferry's identity is a framework for building the global relationships it seeks. It is also a framework for making institutional leadership a way of life that will stand the test of time. How Korn/Ferry satisfies its innate need to help organizations build leadership capital will change at intervals, but its identity will remain immutable, even as the firm continues to grow and evolve.

Embracing this mission also met a key requirement of guiding the firm's transition from founder identity to institutional identity. For instance, because Korn/Ferry's need to build leadership capital was drawn, in part, from Richard Ferry's vision, it tacitly codified many of his characteristics: his deep sense of professionalism, his "global" view of business life, his passion for new knowledge. In addition, using the firm's innate identity as the cornerstone of its mission established an unspoken discipline that would discourage managers from devising strategy that went too far afield from its natural center of gravity. At the same time, it would challenge partners to seek avenues of growth that, as the world changed, would constantly expand on and refresh the original vision of the founders.

The Law of Constancy tells us much about the corporate brand:

- That its definition resides within the identity of the enterprise and cannot simply be fabricated.

- That, as a result, the brand is not transitory, not simply a statement of today's corporate features. Rather, it is timeless in terms of the benefits it yields to those it touches.

- That the brand requires constant reinterpretation.

- That the brand is, or should be, "of the moment" in how it is interpreted.

- That it is vital to establish your own brand "turf" and defend it vigorously, resisting fads, fashions, and others' standards and views, particularly those of competitors.

- That the strengths of the brand develop over time and, to be fully known, must be viewed through the lens of history as well as current events and future aspirations.

In terms of brand management, and overall business management as well, the challenge for all leaders isn't so much to change their organizations. The challenge is to change them in accordance with the identity of a being that is alive in its own right and, on the basis of its innate capacities, knows where it wants to go.

No matter how much success has been achieved and no matter how old the enterprise, the leadership imperative established by the Law of Constancy is to let changes in the outside world spark new ways of expressing the identity within, all in the name of value creation. Forever.

4 THE LAW OF WILL

EVERY ORGANIZATION IS COMPELLED BY THE NEED TO CREATE VALUE IN ACCORDANCE WITH ITS IDENTITY.

I am alive, I am unique, and I am immutable,
even as I grow and evolve.
To truly live, however, I must express
myself fully, *and in this regard, have much*
to give.
But to do so, I need others, and am most productive
with those who need me in return.
To establish these relationships, I must first be
recognized for who I am,
and it follows then that
I will receive in accordance with what I give.

The will to live is often cited as the reason why some people manage to beat the odds. People who have been diagnosed with a terminal disease. People who have been in a serious accident that threatens their life. And people who are simply very old and, as nature would have it, it is their time to die. The will to live is given credit for many things that seem, on the surface, irrational, improbable, and unexpected.

Since the first time I was hospitalized for eye surgery at the age of four, I have struggled to reclaim the person who, in my mind at the time, "tunneled deep" to escape the blinding lights of the operating theater in order to survive. And it is only by sheer force of will, born of my desire to live completely, that I have let nothing get in the way of my ascent from the safety of that dark and silent well. Call it creative problem solving in the extreme. As I have come back, little by little over the years, I have discovered the joy of using my heightened sensitivity to issues of identity to help others comprehend their own. It is how I create value—how I make a proprietary contribution to the world around me.

The will to live is only the most dramatic expression of the fourth Law of Identity, which manifests itself in many other ways in people as well as organizations. The Law of Will may take the shape of the will to break a world record in a marathon, to scale Mount Everest, to be one of the world's "most admired companies," to build the fastest fighter jet in the sky—to be the best at whatever you do, or your company does.

For all the commendable qualities it implies, there is also danger hidden in this fourth Law of Identity. That danger lies in attempting— "willing" yourself—to be something you are not, something that doesn't spring naturally from your identity. I recall how I tried to convince myself after graduate school that retailing was a sensible career path for me. That I quickly lost the job with Filene's was eloquent testimony to the fact that I was operating outside the Law of Will. My rationale was that my father's family had made its living in retailing and that I, like them, had the right genes to succeed. But it was an ill-advised move. I could not "will" myself to succeed, no matter how much I may have wanted to. In similar fashion, you cannot *will* an organization to be something it simply is not. Willpower is effective only when it is exercised in support of the identity of the corporate being involved.

Grit and determination are characteristics we often associate with will, or, more accurately, willpower. Both traits are common to many leaders. In the business landscape, Konosuke Matsushita comes to mind. He reportedly endured a sickly childhood in which he drove himself to survive through persistent hard work. Matsushita went on to found the global organization that carries his name today and, in doing so, helped his employees earn a living even during times when the fate of his company was not at all assured.

In the world at large, figures such as Martin Luther King and Mahatma Ghandi have overcome great odds to achieve extraordinary influence as leaders on behalf of important causes. They have all lived by the Law of Will. Knowingly or not, these people have let their respective identities lead them forward.

The Law of Will contains great passion. It is about determination and courage in the name of accomplishment, most often with benefits to others as well as to oneself. It is first about wisdom, though: knowing what force drives you as an individual—knowing, in fact, that such a force even exists. Some people may choose to ignore this force, but it will not be extinguished.

This wisdom is often tested at the moment when an organization's identity is revealed. That moment can be a crossroads. Taking one direction—letting the identity of the enterprise inform how its future might unfold—can be exhilarating, even liberating. Taking the other direction—denying that identity—is fraught with problems and ultimately costs the firm dearly.

This reality was brought into sharp relief for me in the fall of 1988 as I helped The Upjohn Company (now Pharmacia & Upjohn) take stock of "what made the company special." The assignment represented an important step as management attempted to ready the company to compete in a more complex, global economy.

THE UPJOHN COMPANY

A Campus Perspective

The physical environments of most companies reveal much about who they are. The use of colors, the number (or the lack) of luxury appointments, the type and amount of office space, the quality of everything from plantings to furniture—all say something about the institution. It is the corporate equivalent of how we dress, what our homes look like, and what cars we drive.

The campus of Upjohn's Kalamazoo, Michigan headquarters, like those of many pharmaceuticals companies, was deeply green and meticulously landscaped. The entrance was guarded by a large stone structure that carried the organization's formal name, The Upjohn Company. The use of the article *The*, as I would later realize, was an important clue to the force of will that resided within this institution. Make no mistake about it, this was *The Upjohn Company,* and it had its own way of engaging the world around it.

The beauty of Upjohn's campus was engaging, even seductive. The precision of it all—the clearly bounded expanse of land, the slope of the buildings, the manicured lawns and the pristine courtyards—was welcoming and comforting. It was a serene and ordered place. Perhaps, as I came to see, too serene and too ordered.

Over several months, I began to sense that much was going on beneath the calm of this verdant campus. I imagined that the roots of the trees that lined the many paths, and the rough asphalt underbellies of the driveways that stretched around the circumference of the buildings, reached down to a far different place—a place less serene than what was visible on the surface.

The tranquility of Upjohn's campus was an eerily quiet counterpoint to the intense war of wills that was being waged over the soul of the enterprise. It wasn't a war between rival management factions or between managers from within and without the Upjohn family. It was a war between the will of those who would tie the company's future to a relatively narrow path and the will of the institution itself, whose method of value creation was unquestionably broader.

A Time for Transition

During the period I worked with Upjohn, the company installed its first nonfamily chief executive, Dr. Theodore Cooper. This event brought to the fore questions that had long been begging for answers: What business was Upjohn in? Where did its future lie? And, yes, what made the organization special?

The times seemed to call for symbolic as well as substantive change. Like its pharmaceutical and health care counterparts, Upjohn faced the prospect of doing business in a world that differed dramatically from what it was used to, a world that took the company out of the comfortable isolation that existed within the physical confines of Kalamazoo, Michigan.

The rules of competition were changing. More and more prescription products were being distributed through mass wholesalers, drug chains, and managed health care organizations such as HMOs and directly through corporations to employees. Shorter product life cycles and increasing competition from generic drug alternatives were putting pressure on expected financial returns from proprietary drugs. Increasing consumer awareness and knowledge about medicine and drug purchasing were challenging the tradition of "absolute authority" enjoyed by physicians.

Taken together, the changes Upjohn faced trained a spotlight on four areas the organization had to grapple with. The first was *globalization*—and globalization not simply in terms of physical reach but also in terms of impact. For instance, being fully assimilated into the economic and cultural fabric of ten strategically relevant markets was more valuable than having operations in, or exporting to, fifty different countries.

The second thing Upjohn had to do was find its place in a world increasingly driven by *partnerships* among such previously distinct groups as manufacturers, suppliers, distributors, retailers, and health care professionals. I sensed that becoming more interdependent was a tall order for Upjohn. The company had a strong independent streak and had for decades enjoyed broad-based control over everything from R&D and manufacturing to sales and distribution through physicians.

The third challenge Upjohn faced was *innovation.* Fueled by the need to meet new external realities, managers, investors, and customers all looked to innovation as the lifeblood of success in these uncertain times. The very notion of innovation stirred debate within the enterprise. Some managers saw, and defended, Upjohn as highly innovative. They were quick to cite how the company identified new applications for existing drug formulations, citing *Rogaine* as an example. Others, however, measured innovation in more conventional, pharmaceutical terms—specifically, the development of new proprietary drugs. In this arena, Upjohn's track record was regarded by many "thought leaders" and customers as less than stellar, especially when compared to such companies as Merck and Glaxo.

The fourth area that Upjohn needed to look at with fresh eyes was *quality.* It was axiomatic that quality was important to the drug business—that in terms of efficacy and reliability, quality was essential. But conceiving of quality as a product-related issue was no longer enough. For managers generally, quality had become a matter of overall business performance. In this respect, Upjohn had a ways to go.

Dr. Cooper's appointment was catalytic. For me, his presence served to highlight the company's struggle to figure out what it wanted to be when it grew up. Were Cooper and his team going to up the company's investment in pharmaceuticals research and development? Was the new CEO going to stay the course in animal health, agriculture, and other "non-core" businesses? In the end, would "health care" remain a viable description of the company, or would another way of comprehending what business Upjohn was really in emerge?

The one question that threaded through all of these issues, but was never asked directly, was *What is the will of Upjohn? How is the institution compelled to create value as a result of its identity?* It was my job to ask this central question and to help answer it.

The Climate Within

Upjohn was one of those companies that wore its heritage proudly. Founded by W.E. Upjohn a century earlier, the organization took immense pride in its roots. Upjohn himself was a physician. He was also an inventor. His best-known contribution to medicine was the invention of the friable pill. That is, he discovered a way to produce a pill that would begin to break down and dissolve shortly after it was taken. It was capable of being crushed with the press of a thumb. Up to that time, pills sometimes passed straight through the patient's system without dissolving. The benefits were obvious: The pill was easier on the patient and would release its medicinal properties more consistently.

The friable pill became an icon. It was a symbol of many things: of innovation in drug delivery, of the founder's keen desire to make people's lives easier, and of what healing was all about. The small museum that was part of the Upjohn campus featured many relics and memorabilia of the founder and his family. The satisfaction the company took in the achievements of the past was unmistakable.

From these beginnings, Upjohn grew into one of the most widely respected pharmaceuticals-based health care companies in America. Its family roots were still very much a part of the business when I arrived. William and Donald Parfet, both members of the Upjohn family, occupied senior management positions. Donald Parfet was senior vice president for administration, including strategy, human resources, and communications. Don was my client.

As I got to know the company, I noticed that many managers and employees struggled to articulate their feelings about the heritage of the company and how that heritage was now being played out. One manager in pharmaceuticals marketing earnestly explained that the friable pill "just didn't tell the whole story" and that too much emphasis had come to be placed on the pill alone, at the expense of what the pill signified as a way of caring for patients.

Clearly, there was widespread regard for W.E. Upjohn and for all that he and the Upjohn family had come to stand for. One of the most memorable symbols of this admiration was the dark brown alligator briefcase many people carried. Reminiscent of the one reportedly used by the doctor himself, it was an unmistakable sign that you had made the grade; *you belonged.*

Among the sales force, in particular, the bag was a highly prized status symbol. Receiving one meant that you had reached a certain level of accomplishment in your position. I recall hearing about two Upjohn sales representatives unexpectedly crossing paths in an obscure European airport. It was the first overseas trip for both, and both were carrying their respective alligator bags. Upon catching sight of one another, these two first-time foreign travelers suddenly felt much more at home. For all the positive attributes associated with "the bag," however, I came to see that it was also a sign of membership in a culture that wasn't entirely comfortable in its own skin.

One of the traits ascribed to W. E. Upjohn was a deep and genuine interest in the welfare of his patients—their physical health, but also their mental and emotional well-being. As disingenuous as it may sound in these more cynical times, he cared about them as people and supposedly had a bedside manner to prove it. For a physician, this particular attribute was certainly admirable. By the time I arrived, Doctor Upjohn's reputation had been distilled down to one central characteristic: He was "people-oriented."

Over several generations, this characteristic had been absorbed into the company's bloodstream in ways that were both positive and negative. On the plus side, people were exceptionally considerate of one another. They bent over backwards to not offend each other or say things that might appear overly controversial or threatening. On the minus side, what I came to see as a "polite society" had at times made social performance more important than business performance.

Too Much of a Good Thing

One of the most dramatic examples of this behavior was in how quality was practiced within the company. To its credit, Upjohn's commitment to quality was uncompromising. Producing the "best-quality" products was given high priority. Everyone in the organization took great pride in making drugs that were *superior* in quality to those of competitors. Yet I discovered that this admirable passion also contained hidden problems. The first was that outsiders—customers and investors, in particular—didn't necessarily view offering the best quality as an advantage; in their eyes, the cost of being "the best" actually diminished the attractiveness of some products.

The other problem that stemmed from Upjohn's passion for quality was how it was defined, valued, and lived on a day-to-day basis. About two months into my engagement, I was able to see that the company was operating in line with three very clear but unspoken definitions of quality. These definitions were diverting employees' attention from business performance and refocusing it on social performance.

The first definition was the *quality of products*—most often, how well the product was manufactured. In one of my plant tours, I watched as workers in pale blue sanitary masks and gowns carefully tended the pills that passed down the filling lines. I had been to other such facilities and had witnessed this scene many times before. But this time it was different. Upjohn's passion for quality seemed particularly ritualistic and was manifested in pharmaceuticals that easily met, and often exceeded, FDA standards.

The second definition was *quality of life*—specifically, the environment in which employees worked. Given the beautifully groomed campus, this expression of quality was not surprising to me. The problem came, as I saw it, from the extent to which this value influenced the enterprise. At times I sensed that form reigned over substance. Comfort, and the sometimes genteel pace it engendered, were governing features of the Upjohn culture.

The third way in which quality was expressed was in the *quality of people*. Employee character and dedication to the company were of paramount importance in people's ability to get ahead. Upjohn recruited exceptional people, first-class professionals, whether in sales, marketing, finance, R&D, or manufacturing. For a health care company whose livelihood traded heavily on ethics, moral standards, and "doing the right thing," quality of people mattered greatly. The vulnerability in this last area lay with the fact that this talent wasn't always deployed in the service of improving business performance, especially in making decisions that, though not popular, would enhance the company's ability to compete in a new and unforgiving global world.

How quality came to life at The Upjohn Company didn't tell the whole story. Beneath the social correctness I observed that permeated the culture, Upjohn employees demonstrated a powerful desire to perform—to make change happen, to take chances and make a difference. As I moved from one division to the next, I met with managers, many of whom I felt were potential stars. I spent time with researchers bursting with ideas for new products, and whose belief in those ideas was contagious; young sales representatives who wanted to be far more aggressive in product pricing than was the norm; and finance officers who recognized that the time allotted for return on investment in certain products was unnecessarily long. What was holding these people back?

In one conversation with a marketing manager, I was told that "risk taking is too risky," that mistakes might stay with you for your whole career, and that saying the wrong thing was "a cardinal sin." As I listened to her, I could feel the fear that such a climate might produce in someone. It wasn't the fear of being fired; it was the fear of being ostracized, of not belonging.

Despite this unsettling climate, examples of solid business performance were evident in certain areas. These included pharmaceuticals sales, consumer products, Upjohn Healthcare Services (the company's home health care business), the international division, and fine chemicals. As I quickly saw, these effective operations had one thing in common: They were all close to the customer, where day-to-day interaction governed their success and survival. They were "out there" in the fray. They had left the comfort of the campus behind.

The Law of Will stipulates that *every organization is compelled by the need to create value in accordance with its identity*. The will of Upjohn was alive and well in the pockets of performance that I found throughout the company. I was driven to know more. What was the identity of Upjohn that lay hidden below the surface?

As I considered what I had learned about the culture of Upjohn, my frustration grew. I realized how the organization's interpretation of quality did a disservice to the man who was its progenitor. It was squelching risk taking and innovation. Perpetuating the myth of W.E. Upjohn as *simply* people-oriented detracted from appreciation of his strong views about business. In the written history of the company, I discovered that Doctor Upjohn exhibited characteristics that went to the heart of performance. He was known to be tough but fair. He believed in good business practices, such as making money and being financially disciplined. He espoused the notion that "focus and vision shape performance."

W.E. Upjohn was two things equally. Yes, he was a physician with a deeply felt regard for the welfare of his patients and for people in general. The last thing he might do would be to offend those to whom he ministered. But Upjohn was also a businessman with a healthy respect for business performance. Somehow, over the years, generations of managers had lost sight of this vital second attribute. As I saw it, this lack of understanding was now crippling the company's ability to move forward. The results of this disconnect were apparent. For all its success, the organization lacked self-confidence. People often seemed more concerned with not upsetting one another than with doing the right thing for the enterprise.

My task had been to help figure out what made this company special in order to position Upjohn to compete better globally. By now it was clear to me that no matter what the answer to this question, it wouldn't matter if that answer didn't help to free the organization from a kind of performance paralysis that had set in.

I realized that the solution lay in clarifying the distinctive ways in which the organization created value. Doing so had always helped me put things into perspective for clients, explaining events and circumstances in ways people could understand and deal with. I was convinced that Upjohn was a strong company with a will to match—a will that had lain dormant far too long. How this situation had come about didn't matter; it was time to confront reality.

Thy Will Be Done

The window on the identity of Upjohn was framed by a timely debate over what business the company was in. As I interviewed managers and employees, customers, financial analysts, health care thought leaders and others, the answers to this classic question kept falling into two categories. To many people, Upjohn was a pharmaceuticals company along the lines of Merck, or Glaxo, or Pfizer. Occasional adjectives infused this view with a little more color: Upjohn was a "premier pharma" company; it was an R&D, marketing-based pharma company; it was a direct manufacturer of pharmaceuticals (this means that the company didn't focus on in-licensing other companies' drugs for sale and distribution). Upjohn was in the proprietary drugs business.

The other school of thought was that Upjohn was in the business of medicine and physiology—that it was not limited to pharmaceuticals. It was a distinction with a difference. The individuals I spoke with who held this view (all of them had had long-standing relationships with the company) found unusual ways to make their point. They saw Upjohn as a medical research company, as being in the medical business—a provider of "human medicants," according to one customer. Another said that Upjohn "likes to heal, to cure, not just to make drugs."

It was not surprising to hear these responses from physicians with whom Upjohn had long and deep relationships. I was surprised, however, to get this response from health care administrators. One managed care executive said to me, "They behave like physiologists. They study life and organic systems for medical purposes." On the surface, it was easy to argue that other drug companies also "studied life and organic systems," but that was not what these people were telling me; they were telling me that *Upjohn was different.*

My curiosity grew about these two disparate views of the organization. To help clarify the distinction, I looked up the terms *medicine* and *pharmacology* in the dictionary. The former was defined as "the science and art of dealing with the prevention, cure or alleviation of disease." The latter was defined as "the science of drugs."

As I weighed these two different views, I began to search for clues that would help me better understand *my* patient, Upjohn. It was a pivotal moment because Ted Cooper had already made a key decision: *Upjohn would bet its future largely on pharmaceuticals.* The company would put more money into pharmaceuticals R&D with the aim of developing more proprietary products. New drugs promised high investment returns.

On one hand, this seemed sensible. The company had made money with its drugs and had substantial infrastructure investment in research and development. Further, management had made promises to Wall Street about developing ethical drugs as the basis for increasing

the company's share price. On the other hand, I sensed that this decision might channel resources away from other aspects of the company,
such as home health care, that I suspected were a crucial part of
Upjohn's identity.

I felt that there was more to this organization than was captured
through pharmaceuticals alone. I was concerned that Dr. Cooper's
decision might unwittingly challenge the will of this corporate being
and, in so doing, restrain rather than unleash its ability to create value.

Upjohn's culture was a rich store of information that connected its
past with its present. And it seemed reasonable that this culture also
held clues to its corporate identity. Upjohn's long-standing mission,
"to help mankind through health care," was considered by most
employees to be the cornerstone of Upjohn's culture. Reflecting on this
mission, it seemed to me that it more closely mirrored definitions of
medicine than of pharmacology. Was this connection by design or simply coincidental? Either way, it was a connection that would take on
greater meaning as time passed.

As a first step, I decided to take a closer look at what "medicine"
was all about. What I found were a host of interconnected terms and
ideas that began to tell a vital story about the company. Medicine is
described as the process of dealing with "the maintenance of health
and the prevention, alleviation, or cure of disease." It is all about the
science and art of *healing* and the three basic pillars of healing: diagnosis, prescription, and the administration of medicine.

I realized that this description of medicine suggested a number of
traits characteristic of Upjohn. In everything they did, employees demonstrated a caring attitude and a genuine sense of responsibility for people's
welfare, emotional and mental as well as physical. Compassion and even
empathy were evident in the amount of time people spent talking about
"their patients' self-esteem, along with their function ability." The integration of "high tech" with "high touch" was part of Upjohn's operations, as seen, for instance, through its home health care business.

Each word, in its way, presented a clue. In particular, what exactly
did "healing" mean, and how was that meaning related to Upjohn? As
I read the definition of healing, I believed I was on to something especially important. To "heal" was to make sound or whole, to restore

someone, or something, to its original purity or integrity. The connection between medicine and integrity had not been evident to me until then. The next logical step was to take a closer look at the meaning of integrity, which was one of the features I had already identified in connection with leading organizations, generally.

Integrity is often associated with adherence to a code of values, but it was another meaning that captured my attention. Integrity meant being in an "unimpaired condition," being in a "state of completeness, undivided, fully carried out." Despite the awkwardness of the language, there was something telling about this description in connection with Upjohn.

Another arena for investigation was Upjohn's internal functions, marketing in particular. In order to understand how this corporate being "wanted" to create value, I needed to understand its approach to customers. As I quickly saw, Upjohn's relationships with customers paralleled classic physician–patient interaction. In other words, the relationship wasn't just disease-oriented; it was education-oriented. Upjohn reps loved to educate health care professionals and administrators alike about new drug therapies and various disease states. Upjohn's focus on pharmaceuticals was complemented by its attention to psychology and behavior-related therapies.

Perhaps the most striking aspect of Upjohn's marketing approach was its MSL program—a group of highly trained professionals, or "medical sciences liaisons." MSLs were Upjohn's secret weapon in the battle for market penetration and customer loyalty. As I learned, the success of the MSL program was rooted in, and fueled by, what one physician described as Upjohn's "medical mindset."

MSLs worked alongside what Upjohn managers had identified as the top 1% of physicians and thought leaders. Their job was to develop concepts for new products, to arrange for high-profile speakers, and to sponsor programs that would advance the interests of both the customer and the company. The MSLs were Upjohn's storehouse of knowledge. These scientifically trained professionals could engage in informed discourse about the present—and the future—of medicine. Perhaps most important, MSL's were seen as not having a commercial bias. They were, in essence, Upjohn's *field doctors*.

Upjohn's marketing department had managed to establish an image for the company that went well beyond proprietary pharmaceuticals. The customers, securities analysts, and others I spoke with were quick to point to a variety of distinctive traits. They cited Upjohn's orientation toward combatting the disease rather than just promoting the drug. One physician described how Upjohn seemed to be involved in numerous aspects of medicine, including incidence, prognosis, and epidemiology. A wholesaler remarked that the company was "preoccupied with the human condition and patient welfare." In still other cases, it was clear to outsiders that Upjohn showed a bias toward pure, or basic, medical science over traditional research and development.

It was now clear to me that what made Upjohn *Upjohn* transcended proprietary drugs. A sharp distinction formed in my mind between classic pharmaceuticals innovation (the discovery and formulation of new drug compounds) and what I viewed as medical innovation (the discovery and formulation of new *medical concepts*). On the surface, Upjohn seemed better at the latter than the former. I decided to take a close look at an economic yardstick that might help to illuminate this distinction.

One of the things that fired people's passions at Upjohn was conceiving significant new indications for existing drugs, especially uses that filled therapeutic vacuums in the marketplace. At the time, *Rogaine* was the high-profile example of such "concept formulation." Rogaine is Upjohn's pioneering Minoxidil-based formula that stimulates hair growth in men. Previously, Minoxidil had been used principally to lower blood pressure. Although Rogaine didn't save lives, it did help men save face: It bolstered self-confidence and contributed to self-esteem. I found that every time a new indication such as this came up in conversation, it sparked spontaneous pride and excitement. It was a wake-up call to the corporate spirit.

I soon realized that concept formulation was a world unto itself at Upjohn. It was a world where identifying a condition in need of treatment, and then providing the drugs to alleviate it, were important measures of achievement.

If this type of innovation was so stimulating, what, if anything, was its economic value to Upjohn? Working with managers in pharmaceuticals marketing, I identified six products that, together, told a crucial tale. Each of these products was born of a new *concept's* having been formulated, rather than a new drug. For instance, Upjohn latched on to the concept of "panic disorder"—a condition that, once identified, demanded a cure that Upjohn, as it happened, was fully prepared to deliver.

In each case, we were able to trace the incremental (read "unexpected") revenues Upjohn received from product sales above and beyond anticipated revenues. Over a ten-year period, the all-in number reached nearly $700,000,000. The two most dramatic examples of this dynamic were Xanax, Upjohn's answer to panic disorder, and Cleocin Phosphate, the company's response to anaerobic infection, a condition brought about through a lack of oxygen.

Concept formulation was a crucial expression of what made Upjohn tick. It linked two of the disciplines Upjohn loved best: science and marketing. It was, I believed, the insatiable will of the organization in full bloom. As far as I could see, however, management did not fully appreciate how significant this capacity was.

Some people saw it as just good luck. Others labeled it serendipity. It was neither. Concept formulation and the revenue stream that resulted were a core aspect of how this enterprise created value. I felt that management should institutionalize the process. The opportunity cost of not doing so was high. How could senior Upjohn managers make informed decisions about the direction of the enterprise if they didn't appreciate this central aspect of Upjohn's identity?

The Pieces Come Together

In light of this discovery, I thought about the wisdom of limiting the company's future to proprietary pharmaceuticals. What effect would this decision have on Upjohn's innate passion for concept formulation? How would operating as a classic pharmaceuticals company serve the broader medical will of this corporate being? Why was it so critical to focus only on "the pills"?

This last question led me to think back to the founder's development of the friable pill and the legends that had grown up around it.

Perhaps people had gravitated to the pill as the cornerstone of value creation, rather than to the "science and art of medicine" that was its true foundation.

Producing pills—that is, being in the pharmaceuticals business only—seemed to make perfect sense, but unfortunately, it was out of sync with the will of Upjohn. Focusing on proprietary drugs was also ironic. The long-standing association between W.E. Upjohn and the friable pill actually did an injustice to the founder himself. The pill was simply a tool—a means of helping people. The doctor's relationship with his patients had always gone beyond the drugs he administered. From what I had seen to date, The Upjohn Company shared this broader orientation. A pill may have jump-started The Upjohn Company, but the company had always been more than the pill.

I had begun to piece together elements of the company into combinations that seemed to reveal the special ways in which Upjohn worked. The first such combination did not seem surprising initially. Upjohn's activities in basic and applied research—investigation, insight, and revelation—blended into *scientific discovery*—the "discovery" not only of new compounds but also of new concepts, where new knowledge about disease states and medical conditions was the key deliverable. Scientific discovery at Upjohn seemed to focus on problem *definition*.

A second combination of skills included Upjohn's particular talent for concept formulation (such as its response to the need for a treatment for panic disorder), new-product development, and formulation and production of the drugs themselves, taking into account their efficacy, reliability, and, yes, superior quality in manufacturing. Together, these distinct capacities constituted Upjohn's particular brand of remedy; it was Upjohn's unique "Rx" and it framed the company's passion for *medical innovation*.

A third combination of factors spoke to how Upjohn developed relationships with customers, among them physicians, administrators, and patients. The company's orientation toward customers was caring, professional, and scrupulously honest. An ability to bring new ideas and knowledge to the table also defined these relationships. For example, Upjohn's medical sciences liaisons (MSLs) were a pivotal force in building and sustaining interaction with Upjohn's professional customer base. Another component in the relationship equation was Upjohn's in-home-care services. A stand-alone operation, home health care enabled the company to interact with patients and bring them not only drugs but also psycho-social care through on-site nurses and social workers.

Taken together, these factors produced what I termed Upjohn's *quality interface system*—the distinctive way in which the company engaged the marketplace. *Quality* referred to the superior level and consistency of performance in these interactions. This was one area where the commitment to quality clearly went beyond the products. *Interface* referred to the points where Upjohn people and products met, influenced, and communicated with people and products outside. Examples included the drug–physiology interface, the sales rep–customer interface, the interface between MSL and thought leader, and that between the health care worker (such as a nurse) and the patient. *System* referred to how these various interactions formed an integrated and discernible pattern of behavior.

When I lined up these three combinations—scientific discovery, medical innovation, and the company's quality interface system—I saw how they fused into a unified system for value creation. Upjohn's proprietary contribution in the marketplace was evident in new knowledge about important disease states, in the alleviation of illness through new and existing drugs, and in the company's dedication to the emotional well-being of patients.

Upjohn's return on its investment in value creation—the wealth it received—could be measured in several ways. It could be gauged in terms of sales and earnings growth, return on invested capital, generally (and return on new-concept formulations, specifically), long-term customer loyalty, and awareness and support within the patient population.

The pieces were coming together fast, but I still wasn't satisfied. I still hadn't found words to describe the identity of Upjohn. How exactly was this value creation process related to the company's broad medical orientation? How did it embrace corporate history as well as current events?

All at once I made a critical connection: *Value creation at Upjohn replicated the healing process on a grand scale.* Scientific discovery—investigation, insight, and revelation—was synonymous with *diagnosis.* Medical innovation revolved around *prescription*—the prescription of drugs, yes, and also other therapies reflecting the conviction that self-esteem is as important as physical needs to the quality of life. And Upjohn's quality interface system was all about the *administration* of "medicine" in a variety of forms. I sensed the will of this company straining to make itself known, to be acknowledged, to be exercised. Although pharmaceuticals were a vital part of its make-up, Upjohn was a medical company in the deepest and richest sense.

As I considered the value-creating capacities of Upjohn, I recalled what I had come to understand clearly in my work with Alcoa: that discerning identity is about *seeing through* all the layers—through a company's products and services, through its organizational units, through the tenets of culture that prescribe behavior, through the assumptions about "what business we're in." It is about seeing through all of this until you reach down to the heart, mind, and soul of the company as a self-directing entity in the purest sense. This is where identity lies, I thought, moving to its own rhythm, unencumbered by all the layers that distract managers from what really "makes the company tick."

As I reflected on this reality, I thought about the parallels between Upjohn and the definitions I had found when I analyzed the meanings of the words *medicine, physician,* and *healing* in particular—of making things whole and complete. I finally had the answer I was looking for. Upjohn was driven by the need to *restore and maintain the integrity of human life.* The organization had a burning desire to heal the whole person. This, I realized, is what made Upjohn special. This was, indeed, *The* Upjohn Company.

The implications of the Law of Will were unseen by management. The organization's drive to create value *its way* was in conflict with leadership whose intent, no matter how economically rational, was discordant with the identity of the organization.

The Laws of Identity recognize nothing but the truth. Upjohn was born to create value by exercising its deep-seated need to restore and maintain the integrity of human life. The fact that Upjohn was alive— a self-directing being with a mind of its own—was, for me, an established fact when I began my assignment. For this great American company to thrive, especially, under the rules of global competition, it had to express itself fully. That was the only way it could hope to meet these new rules on acceptable terms.

A MATTER OF PRIORITIES

The conversations I had with management about the unique capacities of the enterprise were animated. Some executives, notably Don Parfet and other members of his team, were intrigued by what they heard. For them, this discovery touched a chord. Other executives were reluctant to accept my characterization of Upjohn's identity and what it implied about the direction and future investment imperatives for the organization.

The Upjohn Company had stood as one of America's most highly regarded business success stories for over a century. Despite this success, I believe that its merger with Pharmacia in 1995 was inevitable. On the surface, the merger occurred because of Upjohn's less than stellar financial performance at the time. But below the surface, I believe that the company's demise as an independent enterprise was predictable because management had failed to heed the voice of the organization.

From my vantage point, the decision to make classic pharmaceuticals R&D Upjohn's center of gravity weakened the enterprise, constraining rather than liberating value. The net result of ignoring identity was a depressed stock price that set the stage for the merger. Although investors may not have understood the picture in its entirety, they certainly understood its ramifications.

In the year I worked with Upjohn, I came to see great vitality in the people I met and their commitment to the company. Upjohn, the corporate being, was very much alive, but it had never been given a chance to express itself on its own terms. Was this the fault of the executive team at that time? Only superficially. It was probably the result of managers seeking, for years, to turn Upjohn into something that it essentially was not. Consider it a case of mistaken identity. Narrowing its strategy to focus on designing, developing, and marketing new drugs was not enough to make Upjohn a full-fledged, R&D-driven, pharmaceuticals company.

There is no doubt that for then-CEO Theodore Cooper, and others, to have seriously considered the profound impact of the will of the organization on its future would have entailed risk and required great courage. Liberating the company's identity implied many prospective changes—in investment strategy, in business composition, in recruiting and training, in almost every area of the enterprise. But then courage in the name of integrity is what the Law of Will demands.

In connection with the discipline of leadership, the fourth Law of Identity clarifies priorities in no uncertain terms: *Identity precedes strategy*. It never works the other way around. If strategy, vision, mission, or purpose is to have staying power, then it must flow from identity.

5 THE LAW OF POSSIBILITY

IDENTITY FORESHADOWS POTENTIAL.

I am alive, I am unique, and I am immutable,
even as I grow and evolve.
To truly live, however, I must express myself fully,
and in this regard, have much to give.
But to do so, I need others, and am most productive
with those who need me in return.
To establish these relationships, I must first be
recognized for who I am,
and it follows then that
I will receive in accordance with what I give.

The Law of Possibility marks a turning point in the road prescribed by the Laws of Identity. Building on the strength and momentum of the laws that precede it, this fifth law becomes a window on the future of an organization in ways that reveal its potential for timeless value creation.

Potential based on identity comes in many forms. There is the potential for discovering and pursuing new avenues of growth. There is the potential for smoothing the path to change by showing employees how the past, the present, and the future are all anchored by identity. There is the potential for healing—for restoring people's faith that there *is* a viable future in the wake of a crippling operating, environmental, or financial crisis.

The Law of Possibility bridges discovery and transformation—the discovery of identity and the rich prospects for transformation that are contained within it. It is a critical juncture. Although the possibilities for growth that stem from identity can be dramatic, they can also produce discomfort: A kind of mental cold sweat breaks out when we find ourselves facing a life-changing decision. Why is this? It is because the extraordinary opportunities inherent in identity do not come easily or cheap. It is because they shake up the status quo.

None of this, however, changes the fact that the Law of Possibility is with us every moment of our lives as individuals and throughout the lives of the corporate beings we create and work with. We are, in essence, *born* into it, and once we have embraced the Law of Possibility as a framework for growth, there is no going back.

Knowing your potential is one of the most powerful forces on earth. To be able to see what *might become* as a direct result of your unique characteristics—how you might affect the world and how the world might respond—is exhilarating. In practical terms, being able to envision the future gives leaders a platform from which to organize everything they and their organizations do, from that day forward, to realize that potential.

If there is a hidden flaw in managers' well-intended attempts to transform their organizations, it is that their efforts may lack a clear and compelling picture of what the world might look like as a result of change. I often find that the party line is "The world is changing too fast to know" and that, as a result, "Agility is everything." But painting a picture of what the future might look like in simple, human terms can be the leader's greatest single gift to a confused, often frightened, organization.

In this vein, a company's true identity is a manager's most trustworthy ally. For managers, as for all other employees, to understand the value-creating potential inherent in the identity of their organization is to lay the foundation for constructive change. Why? Because the Law of Possibility excludes no one and offers a sense of hope—for higher growth, for improved morale, for deserved recognition—for all. It is an exquisitely human promise that is as meaningful to individuals as it is to organizations.

Very soon after I joined Anspach Grossman Portugal, I realized that I had found a home, not simply in relation to the firm, but also within myself. I had found a comfort zone in which I felt naturally powerful and confident. Identity, in all its dimensions, was a playing field I understood instinctively, a platform from which to give my gifts. The Army slogan "Be All That You Can Be" took on new meaning for me that has only deepened with time.

On a plane ride from Dallas to New York in 1983, I was traveling with Russ Anspach, one of the founders of AGP and the man who became my mentor. We were talking about the implications of an assignment we had just completed for BOC Health Care, a $1 billion subsidiary of The BOC Group. (The Group is parent to BOC Gases, the second-largest industrial gases company in the world.) Our task had been to help sort out thirty-one different health care businesses and product lines.

I was feeling especially good about myself. BOC represented one of the first large-scale international identity assignments I had led, and so far, the client was pleased. What made the experience particularly gratifying was the then-unusual approach I had taken to the assignment. Along with my analysis of customer and manager perceptions, I had created a psychographic profile of each of four main operations: life support systems, anesthetic pharmaceuticals, home health care, and intravenous products.

Each profile included the underlying *business psychology* of each division (the human dynamics of manufacturing, for instance, differed from the human dynamics of R&D–based businesses); *culture*, or "behavior"; and the *identity characteristics* that "motivated," or gave rise to, that behavior.

Russ noted that the identity characteristics, in particular, could be used to guide naming, branding, and communications decisions. But I saw other possibilities. It seemed to me that the attributes that made BOC Health Care special should be used as criteria for recruiting the right people, developing training curricula, and defining and introducing new values that would build bridges among BOC Health Care's diverse operations. The possibilities, I felt, were extraordinary.

As much as I had come to trust Russ, I was hesitant to share my thoughts and enthusiasm. At the time, most people equated identity with names, logotypes, and design systems, and I wasn't sure how Russ would react. I was afraid that he would regard my ideas as "over the top" or even irrelevant.

As we sat there, my calm exterior betrayed nothing of the tumult inside. On the one hand, I could choose stay the safe course and reveal nothing. I had begun to establish myself at AGP and didn't want to jeopardize my newly found sense of belonging. I knew that once I said what was on my mind, there was no going back. On the other hand, I believed I had much to give and wanted to express what I was thinking.

And so I did. Russ said nothing. He just listened in his usual, intensely thoughtful way. Then he looked over at me. After a second's pause, he finally spoke. "When it comes to identity," he said, "clients often put too much emphasis on the wrong things, such as the logo or the name."

In that moment, my fears dissolved. I felt both relieved and exhilarated. I was also somewhat taken aback by Russ's statement; after all, AGP made money largely through naming and design. But that no longer mattered. I took Russ's words as encouragement to trust my instincts. It was OK for me to push the envelope of "identity consulting." I look back upon that brief experience as a moment of validation. The time had come for me to step up and step out as simply myself; I could begin to breathe my own air.

For the first time, I could envision how my life might unfold professionally. I could see myself working with clients on projects where identity became the fulcrum for growth and contribution, not simply for shaping image. The possibilities contained in identity—a company's or an individual's—are virtually endless. It is a matter of vision, of "seeing" the implications. It wasn't until I had reached my early forties that I began to see the potential inherent in my own identity as both strategist and humanist—and as a lover of all things creative.

One of the aspects of identity that allows it to foreshadow potential is that *identity transcends everything*. It fuses and reveals the particular skills, talents, and passions that make each of us unique. It does this in the corporate world by breaking through the thick cloud banks that can obscure managers' vision. These "clouds" are everywhere: lines of business, organization structure, functions, economic assumptions, budget requirements, products and services, geography, even politics and turf.

In similar fashion, identity breaks through the clouds that obscure our ability as individuals to see our own unique capacities. These clouds too come in many forms: others' views of "who we are," over-identification with our jobs, family expectations, peer pressure, fear of the unknown.

For people and companies alike, identity is the purest representation of the potential for creating value—for making a proprietary contribution to the world we live in. The particular challenge facing managers is to liberate their company's identity in the face of the physical, financial, and social impediments that are obstacles to growth.

Nowhere was this management challenge more apparent than in Westinghouse's Advanced Industrial Systems business unit (AIS) in

1987. Looking back, I now see my engagement with AIS (one of several for Westinghouse) as a microcosm of the corporation's larger struggle to come to terms with its own identity and the unrealized potential it contained.

WESTINGHOUSE — ADVANCED INDUSTRIAL SYSTEMS

A Meeting for Hope, June 1987

The room was in the bowels of one of Westinghouse's facilities just outside the city limits of Pittsburgh. The meeting was already under way when I arrived late, the victim of a delayed flight. The space was packed with several dozen managers of various ranks and ages who represented each of the operations that made up the business unit then known as Advanced Industrial Systems. As I surveyed the group, I noticed the uncanny similarities among the men (there were, at most, half a dozen women) who occupied the gray steel chairs planted evenly throughout the room. It was a sea of people in white shirts with rolled up sleeves, many sporting shirt pocket protectors—the unmistakable badge of the engineer.

John Yasinsky stood behind a floor-level podium in the front of the room addressing the group. I had been working with John and his team for three months at this point. I knew exactly what he was going say, so my focus was on the audience. I watched as this collection of Westinghouse veterans—fifteen years of employment was about average—listened intently. John was talking about the future, about the possibility of even *having* a future, which frankly was not at all certain.

As I watched the event unfold, it looked like a silent movie of a prayer meeting, with each of these several dozen managers nodding silently as they hung on John's words. For several moments, I heard nothing but saw much. The visual effect was intense. All at once, in my mind, these sixty or so men and women became indistinguishable. They blended into one individual whose career, whose passion for the company, whose skills, and whose ability to continue to work rested on what Yasinsky was saying.

I knew that the potential for achieving profitable growth was enormous. And that's what John was talking about. As I watched from the doorway, I imagined Yasinsky at the helm of a ship addressing his crew amid rough seas. At that moment, he was speaking about the newly revealed identity of AIS and the potential it held for "turning the ship." John had found his compass. The only question now was whether he would have enough time to lock his ship onto the course it indicated.

The Assignment

I began working with AIS in March 1987. Westinghouse corporate executives wanted to see whether an "identity review" could help Yasinsky and his group meet three urgent and interdependent challenges. The first was to *expand beyond traditional areas,* such as utilities, into higher-value-added industrial, commercial, and professional markets. The second challenge was to *build a leadership reputation* externally, in those markets deemed strategically important, and internally, as a principal profit and growth center for Westinghouse. The third challenge was to *foster a more unified culture* within AIS.

The climate within AIS when I arrived was both hopeful and fearful. The hope was palpable in many ways. Numerous managers chose to be optimistic and refused to be discouraged by the difficult prospects they faced. They were prepared not to view past business and economic problems as insurmountable. There was also great pride among these people—pride in the fact that AIS represented long-standing, highly regarded Westinghouse businesses.

Fear was equally palpable. A large number of employees were worried about job security. Unlike their more upbeat counterparts, they were pessimistic and doubted that "anything could be done" to save the unit. They saw difficulties encountered in the past as barriers to future success. Yes, these people were proud of their heritage, but they feared it had become an albatross around their necks.

Value Creation from the Ground Up

I knew that in order to understand the identity of AIS, I had to circumvent the waves of emotion that were running both high and low within the business unit. The best way to do this, I realized, was to analyze the particular capabilities of each of the five divisions of AIS and then to put it all together. Each, I hypothesized, would provide clues to how that division created value and, by extension, to the value creation process of AIS as a whole. Despite the fact that I had successfully employed this approach before, I was operating on faith. I had no idea whether the pieces would add up to something significant or reveal a business unit that held no material value and should be broken up.

The first division I studied was Engineering and Instrumentation Services. E&ISD was built on outstanding problem-solving skills that I discovered were supported by a number of attributes. One was a diagnostic mentality whereby managers would challenge customers' own views and think, as one customer put it, "about what is really wrong," before going to work on the problem. Another trait was the division's ability to help build a customer's business by getting deeply involved with helping a customer actually do his or her job. A third key attribute was the division's integrated technical skills based on what I saw as its engineering passion. Engineering was like a religion at E&ISD. It was a "technical creed" that led managers, for instance, to study separate pieces of equipment as an integrated system in order to solve problems supposedly associated with only one.

E&ISD distinguished itself on the strength of exceptional problem-solving skills. The managers who had forged the business took a holistic view of customers' needs and brought to the table what came to be called, internally, "mobile knowledge." The business opportunity suggested by what I had found was for the division to stop selling "parts and process" and start selling the value and benefits it supplied. This wasn't, I thought, so much the "engineering and instrumentation services" business of AIS; it was, more accurately, about *integrated technical services.*

The second division I looked at, Major Mechanical and Electrical Services, was distinguished by its technical dexterity. This central capability was supported by managers' combined know-how about motors, technology, and systems—a turnkey mentality about how pieces of equipment work together—that set their repair skills apart from others. Another hallmark was the division's ability to do large-scale jobs on very short notice. Several customers acknowledged to me that

Westinghouse was number one when it came to putting a S.W.A.T. team together to deal with "big problems fast."

What MMES did was to keep industry up and running with little or no down time. Thanks to its superior repair capabilities, the division was poised to identify and capitalize on niche opportunities where it could achieve a premium for the comfort and assurance it offered. What business was this division in? Simply put, it was in the business of *industry support services.*

The third operation was the Combustion Control Division (CCD), a business centered on combustion analyzers, principally for industrial boilers. Westinghouse's distinctive capability in this area was how it blended "best" technology with its applications expertise. CCD analyzers were widely known to offer superior sensitivity and stability. Customers also knew, and relied on, Westinghouse's general research and development base, which had links to the division. I finally understood the extent of the division's applications skills when a customer commented that "Westinghouse people could sit on my side of the table as well as their own."

CCD was well positioned to extend its reach from combustion control into unrelated businesses such as ultrasonics and renewal parts. In terms of strategic growth, this AIS operation seemed poised also to expand on the whole concept of analytical instrumentation. It was outstanding at the business of *analytics,* a term that best captured the value-creating potential of the division.

The fourth AIS division I assessed was what was known as Automation, or, more specifically, process control. Customization was Automation's distinguishing strength against such competitors as Foxboro and Bailey. Automation had the seemingly unique ability to configure for customers a system that met their exact needs with little change or special effort in their manufacturing system. Three characteristics supported this capability: Westinghouse's strong technology skills, its systems orientation, and what I saw as the division's "science and art" attitude toward the business of automation.

Competition in this arena was fierce, and it was agreed that the division needed to protect its utility market share. At the same time, however, the skills, experience, and convictions of the people engaged in this operation suggested an opportunity to move the business forward. To do so, managers needed to see that the real strength of the division was in overall *process management*—Westinghouse process management, to be precise—not simply manufacturing automation.

The last division I evaluated was Westinghouse Motor Company. Of all the operations within Advanced Industrial Systems, "Motor" was in the greatest economic trouble. It was struggling to stay profitable.

Despite the precariousness of this division's economic health, the motor operation had discernible strengths. These included customization through engineering (they knew how to "work the motor" to fit customers' needs), quality manufacturing (the integrity of a Westinghouse motor was never challenged), and after-market service and support. The division was also praised for its field support and emergency assistance. For customers, the net benefits of doing business with the motor company were reliability, greater manufacturing and process output, and superior design information.

If sustained profitability was to be achieved, division managers needed to stop taking for granted their single greatest asset: Westinghouse design and engineering and their ability to customize solutions around it. *"Industry motors"* was a legitimate, though struggling, competence of the business unit that seemed, if properly positioned, to have room to grow.

On the surface, then, AIS was an unglamorous collection of businesses, some making decent returns, others not. Moreover, the connections among these businesses were not at all apparent. Under the surface, however, I was able to discern four distinct capabilities that all operations shared and that framed the value-creating potential of the business unit.

First, these seemingly disparate businesses all demonstrated *a problem-solving approach* to interaction with customers; professional objectivity, coupled with empathy for the customer, permeated the place. Second, the five divisions all took *a holistic view of their customers' needs*; it wasn't the piece of equipment or the process that was important but how these things worked together. Third, managers across all operations exhibited an almost *obsessive concern with the customer's welfare* and strove to have a fundamental impact on that customer's business—on its very ability to perform. Finally, all divisions within AIS showed *a deep regard for technology generally, and for engineering in particular*. It was a passion that ran in the blood of Westinghouse.

The identity of the business unit, which had been buried under a mound of "parts and processes," suddenly became crystal clear: *AIS was distinguished by its passion for the science of industry*. The "science" was visible in the unit's investment in technology-driven, higher-margin businesses where Westinghouse brought, or planned to purchase, proprietary knowledge and skills. The notion of "industry" spoke to managers' aggressive pursuit of markets beyond utilities and even beyond industrial customers. On another plane, I realized that the unit's focus on industry, generally, was a proxy for its deep desire to make a difference—with customers, with its customers' customers, and by extension in the society to which Westinghouse had contributed for decades.

To articulate the identity of AIS was to reveal its potential to create value as a single, optimally integrated organization. Its passion for the science of industry, as prescribed by its innate capabilities, pointed the way toward a future that I saw as far brighter than what others had come to believe was possible. AIS was anything but dead. It was very much alive with a great deal to give to the world around it.

John Yasinsky was taken by this characterization of the identity of his unit. He was, I believe, compelled by its simplicity, its logic, and the truth it contained. He began talking in terms of the business's "focus on the science of industry," infusing it into the marketing, sales, and communications fabric of the group. In my conversations with John, he seemed to understand that the potential for building the division around its identity was enormous. In practical terms, for instance, it implied criteria for investing in those divisions—more precisely, in those capabilities—that could contribute the most to furthering the higher-margin, "scientific" content of their operation.

At one point, managers started to forecast the future of the business unit squarely in light of its identity. One document read, "In terms of direction, the business unit is refining its science-of-industry strategy by pursuing more highly differentiated, higher-margin markets where proprietary knowledge shapes competitive advantage." It was essentially these ideas, framed in a simpler, jargon-less way, that

John Yasinsky offered as he addressed the dozens of managers who filled that basement room in a facility outside Pittsburgh that day in June of 1987.

Along with the window it opened on strategy, AIS's innate identity suggested something else that I believe was even more important at the time: a shared sense of purpose that was sorely needed to help the unit coalesce as one enterprise. As much as it suggested a path to profitable growth, AIS's identity was also a leadership platform for John Yasinsky—a place to stand that naturally embraced and linked all five operations, while allowing each to operate according to its own business requirements.

The identity of AIS revealed how, by better understanding its value creation process, the unit might grow beyond utilities and other industrial arenas into higher-value-added markets. AIS's identity—its passion for the science of industry—also provided a framework for building a leadership reputation and a more unified culture through which to pursue growth.

Under the Law of Possibility, it is axiomatic that the whole of any organization is greater than the sum of its parts. The challenge is to *see through* the parts to the whole. Advanced Industrial Systems was the beneficiary of this process in 1987. It is equally true that, in terms of value, pursuing the prospective benefits inherent in the whole far outweighs the short-term comforts derived from maintaining and protecting the status quo. Under John Yasinsky's leadership, AIS was poised to succeed.

A PSYCHO-SOCIAL FRAMEWORK

It is impossible for me to consider the Law of Possibility and its impact on the lives of individuals and companies, AIS included, without thinking about the combined work of Erik Erikson and Abraham Maslow. Abraham Maslow is best known for conceiving the hierarchy of needs. This is a construct, in the form of a pyramid, that demonstrates how people ultimately aspire to *self-actualization*; once their basic needs are met, they strive to reach their potential.

It is useful to review the pyramid briefly, for it reflects the needs of every corporate being as well as every human being. The base of the pyramid reflects our *physiological* needs—we need health, food, and shelter as a prerequisite to living. The next step up the pyramid is *safety*—the need to feel safe in the world, not anxious or fearful. The third level reflects our *social* needs—the need for belonging to a family, a team, a company, or society. The fourth level of the pyramid consists of our need for *self-esteem*. In essence, we need to feel loved and respected, needed and important, and genuinely worthy of all of this. At the top of the pyramid is our need for *self-actualization*.

The development of a business institution and its resulting performance in many ways mirror this same hierarchy. In order simply to survive, an organization must have certain basic needs met; for instance, it needs cash and capital. The organization then needs to feel confident about its particular place in its industry or market. It needs, as well, to feel part of a community of peers. Beyond this, organizations need to be respected by others. And finally, like the people who populate them, they need to be all they are capable of being—they need to *self-actualize*.

The Laws of Identity, and the Law of Possibility in particular, reinforce the inescapable relevance to organizations of Maslow's hierarchy of needs (self-actualization is all about potential). But they do so fully only in light of Erik Erikson's views of human life. Among his many works, Erikson's *Identity and the Life Cycle* captures three ideas that speak most eloquently to the link between identity and leadership. In a chapter entitled "The Healthy Personality," Erikson coins the term *generativity*. What he is referring to, essentially, is parenting: people's drive to produce and care for offspring. As Erikson explains it, generativity concerns establishing and guiding the next generation.

Erikson next delves into *integrity*, building his description aptly on generativity. Erikson's view is that only individuals who have in some way taken care of others, and who have managed to adapt themselves to the "triumphs and disappointments of being the originator of others and generator of things and ideas," can lay claim to having integrity. Erikson's words reflect as much passion as intellect. He goes on to talk about how people with integrity are "ready to defend the dignity of their own lifestyles against all physical and economic threats." Then Erikson addresses leadership directly. He speaks about how integrity (more specifically, *ego integrity*) relies on being emotionally at peace with yourself. This opens the door for others to follow you, while you accept the responsibility of leadership.

Finally, Erikson addresses *identity* head on. He sees identity as the integration of two things. The first is an individual's link with the distinctive values of his or her people (his or her family, history, and heritage). *The second component of identity is related to the individual's* unique development—the traits that make each of us special.

All of these points are relevant to how organizations are managed today. For instance, generativity implies the need for stewardship—for managers to be guardians of the future as well as the present. Integrity speaks to managing through crisis and change and coming out whole, ready to lead. Erikson's view of identity, in the context of business, describes the successful integration of individuality and history into a unique corporate being.

This synthesis of Maslow's description of self-actualization and Erikson's views of human behavior brings us back to the definition of value that is at the heart of identity-based management: Value is the proprietary contribution a company is *capable* of making in the marketplace. It is a definition that fuses the identity of an organization with its environment by revealing the potential benefits of identity to all stakeholders, including society at large. This definition of value is particularly telling in relation to the larger Westinghouse story.

AIS was a product of the Westinghouse culture. Not simply in terms of the corporation's great engineering competence but also in a negative way, in relation to its near obsession with short-term financial performance. In a critical speech delivered to senior managers shortly after I completed my assignment with AIS, two senior corporate officers spoke about putting Westinghouse on a path to "greatness." They compared the organization to the likes of Caterpillar, IBM, Marriott, and Heinz. Their basis for comparison was *return on equity*. Their goal was to achieve an ROE comparable to that of institutions of this stature. Although revenue growth was a factor, their plan relied primarily on judicious cost management as a way to reach their targets as quickly as possible. As I read this speech in advance of its delivery. I knew that neither of these executives understood the fundamentals of value creation.

For all of John Yasinsky's determination and fortitude, the cards were stacked against him and his organization. As was implied in this speech, the future was not as "material" as the present. What was expected of AIS was smart cost reduction; organizational uniqueness and history were beside the point. In the end, the Advanced Industrial Systems unit of Westinghouse was dissolved and the pieces either sold or spun off—the tragic undoing of an organization's productive potential.

REALIZING POTENTIAL

The Law of Possibility challenges conventional thinking. It requires us to view life through a lens that is alien to most individuals and business managers. Instead of looking at the world from the outside in, the fifth law of identity demands that we look at things from the inside out. Constructing this view may well require input from such "outsiders" as suppliers, customers, and investors. But once our view is clear, once identity is known, it is time to reevaluate things in their entirety. The Law of Possibility offers us a unique framework for imagining our destiny.

At various moments, every manager who wishes to lead must peer through the lens provided by identity—his own as well as his organization's. It is the way of renewal, of shaking off the assumptions and beliefs that constrain innovation and change and limit our ability to see.

In business, and often in life, we tend to follow a linear, left-brain path. Why? Because that course appears safe, understandable, known. But when it comes to capturing the potential inherent in one's identity— or in the identity of one's organization—what is already known and perceived as safe often leads nowhere. "Known quantities," in the form of data, facts, empirical evidence, and observable behaviors, reflect at best where we've been and who we are. They say little about what *might* be.

Managers who strive to capitalize on the potential of the enterprise as a whole may also encounter resistance from the way their companies are organized—by functions, by divisions, by geographies, by product lines. Fragmentation undoes cohesion. The magnificent possibilities inherent in the whole are sacrificed to the agendas of the parts.

To understand identity's potential requires large doses of right-brain, whole-being thinking on the part of managers and their teams. It is the art and science of disciplined, creative analysis aimed at designing an organization almost from the ground up. The vital question that reveals identity's value-creating potential is *"If X, then what?"* If AIS is truly distinguished by its focus on the science of industry, if Upjohn is truly driven by a need to restore and maintain the integrity of human life, if Fidelity Investments has a pervasive need to celebrate individualism, *then what are the implications* for the enterprise? For strategy? For organization structure? For marketing, sales, and customer service? For training and development? For investment spending and budgeting? For reward and recognition? For hiring and firing? The possibilities are endless. There is no function, no division, no job, no individual, no future that is beyond a world illuminated by identity.

One of the facts of corporate life illuminated by the Law of Possibility is that unmet potential is a universal reality for all companies. There is always more to do, and always more to be, as an organization's identity is brought to life.

Along with the extraordinary opportunities offered by the Law of Possibility comes the attendant responsibility to pursue those opportunities, but to pursue them in a disciplined way. What this amounts to is the responsibility to *reach for the stars with both feet on the ground*.

The potential that identity holds can be realized in many ways. Sometimes these ways are grand: the revitalization (more accurately, the liberation) of Disney that occurred under Michael Eisner in his early years as chief executive; the unrelenting march of Microsoft as it forges new ways of life for all of us. At other times the realization of potential is more modest and systemic.

Increasing consolidation in the automotive industry today, for instance, suggests that a more dynamic role may be in store for corporate brands such as General Motors, Toyota, Ford, and DaimlerChrysler. If so, then what are the inherent benefits of these names to consumers? What value does each corporate brand convey?

As I consider this issue today, I am reminded of a concept so effectively used by American Express: the idea that *membership has its privileges*. Perhaps this notion is perfect for the car company of tomorrow. Perhaps one of these global leaders will figure out how to charge consumers an annual fee just for the privilege of belonging to the family. In return, the institution would provide its "members" with special discounts on all its product brands, along with a host of value-added services, such as financing, insurance, and roadside assistance. The value created for the customer would be concrete, and the *return on value creation*, very high. The fascinating question is "Which organization, on the basis of its innate identity, is best positioned to pull this off?" Which one has the roots, the passion, the *instinctive need* to make this happen?

The Law of Possibility has one central aim: to liberate the productive potential inherent in identity, whether an individual's or a company's. Yet identity doesn't lay out an exact path; what it provides is *direction*. Both human and corporate beings must then weigh the risks and rewards of each of the choices that identity offers.

It makes no sense, for instance, for a business institution to pursue avenues that may threaten the economic soundness of the enterprise. At the same time, what constitutes "economic soundness" may need to be reassessed in light of identity. Longer payback periods and different rates of return may be called for, given the governing influence that identity exerts on the long-term welfare of an organization.

It is of no value to glimpse the possibilities if we turn away from them in the end. Leadership is about enabling the organization to achieve self-actualization, to reach its potential through relentless value creation. The notion that life can be a self-fulfilling prophecy is borne out within the context of the fifth Law of Identity. So is the fact that we are all in a position to shape our own destinies and the destinies of the organizations we serve.

6 THE LAW OF RELATIONSHIP

**ORGANIZATIONS ARE INHERENTLY
RELATIONAL, AND THOSE RELATIONSHIPS
ARE ONLY AS STRONG AS THE NATURAL
ALIGNMENT BETWEEN THE IDENTITIES
OF THE PARTICIPANTS.**

*I am alive, I am unique, and I am immutable,
     even as I grow and evolve.*
*To truly live, however, I must express myself fully,
     and in this regard, have much to give.*
**But to do so, I need others, and am most
     productive with those who need me
     in return.**
*To establish these relationships, I must first be
     recognized for who I am,
          and it follows then that*
I will receive in accordance with what I give.

Before you can be comfortable with others, you must first be comfortable with yourself. This fact goes to the heart of the first two Laws of Identity, the Law of Being and the Law of Individuality, and all things flow from it. To "know thyself," as Socrates said, is the prerequisite to living a life of integrity where things fall into place naturally.

It is equally true that we need others in order to live. Realizing an individual's or a company's potential—that of Westinghouse's, for instance—isn't done in a vacuum. It is not a solitary act. It demands the participation of others, especially others for whom your value-creating gifts, or those of your company, hold special meaning.

It is not that we need others to define us or to affirm our worth; we need others to let us to be who we are. On its own, the potential inherent in my identity doesn't amount to much. My wife and my son, however, play important roles as "recipients" of my identity—of the things I have come to know about life and living, of my continuing love for art in the form of photography and music. In turn, I do not take for granted the honor of being the recipient of the many things that flow from *their* unique identities. So it is with my friends, who respond to my gifts and whose gifts, in return, I cherish.

When it comes to successful relationships, we often speak of the indefinable magic that forms an invisible bond as "chemistry." We also blame chemistry for bad relationships. I believe that what we call chemistry is really the result of the natural alignment between the identities of two or more beings, whether they are humans or organizations. One of the principal "payoffs" from this alignment is how it accelerates the individual's ability to be more of who he or she (or it) really is.

Mary Kay Ash's relationship with the employees of the company she founded, Mary Kay Cosmetics, is perhaps best measured by the number of pink Cadillacs awarded to salespeople (men and women) who meet or exceed their quotas. That car is a crucial bridge between this CEO and her organization. It is a symbolic bond between individuals who need each other. Not "need" in the sense of weakness, but need in terms of their dependence on each other to fire up the vital capacity to develop, make, and sell cosmetics they really believe in. It is a need the sales representatives must meet in order to be productive.

A similar bond exists between Mary Kay sales associates and consumers. It is fair to say that there is an intimate relationship between salesperson and customer and that every time a customer applies a Mary Kay product, the founder is present in spirit. The value that Mary Kay Ash has created for others comes largely from being more of who she naturally is. The same can be said of the company's salespeople. The same can be said of the company itself.

I met my wife, Janet, at Carnegie-Mellon University in 1971. We were married in the spring of 1975. Jan's background was classically corporate. Her father worked for Westinghouse. She received her M.S. in industrial administration from Carnegie-Mellon. At the same time, there was little emphasis on culture and the arts in her family. Not so in my case; both of my parents were passionate about classical music and foreign travel. Like Jan, I was drawn to the corporate world as a career path, but I knew little about it because my father's background was in small, entrepreneurial businesses.

Our marriage brought together many things that constituted "gifts" to one another: Jan's ability to help educate me about the world of big business; my ability to show her the world of Beethoven and Mozart via Tanglewood, the summer home of the Boston Symphony Orchestra. The more I gave her in the form of those things I knew well and loved, the more I was being truly "productive." I was creating value in the deepest sense.

As I have come to understand the Law of Relationship, I have also come to regret even more my father's death when I was twenty-five. One of the results of my eye operation at the age of four was that I developed a severe distrust of my father. As I drifted, terrified, into sleep under the influence of ether, I imagined that the surgeon who loomed over me was my father, who now wanted to change me, for what reason I could not fathom. It took me until I was twenty-seven—two years after he died—to realize what I had unconsciously done.

Whatever relationship we might have developed was sharply curtailed, not only by his untimely death but also by my terrible, unwitting fantasy. I will never fully know the things—the good and the bad—that made us, finally, of one blood. I do know that, as much as we were different, we were also much the same.

I cannot say that my father was the strategist that I have become, but I know that he was very much a humanist in his own way: a lover of the earth, his family and friends, gardens and nature, and music. He was a man of serious passions, many of which we shared. On this level our identities were quite naturally aligned. We enjoyed many moments together fishing on Stockbridge Bowl, the lake that lies just below Tanglewood. In these moments, which serenity made for me almost timeless, I felt as though my father and I were simply one person. All my fear slipped away as I netted his bass, or as he helped me untangle a knot in my line.

Unfortunately, the "productivity" of our relationship was a shadow of what it might have been. The thousands of conversations that never took place, and the joy that I believe this relationship would have produced, have only served to crystallize for me one of the central aspects of the Law of Relationship: *that individuals most need those who need them in return.* Organizations are no different.

FROM VALUE CREATION TO THE VALUE CIRCLE

The Law of Relationship supplies a model that illustrates how this basic human equation works for business institutions. The model, which I call the *value circle*, addresses value creation through the eyes of all stakeholders, revealing, in particular, the inviolable cause-and-effect relationship among employees, customers, and investors.

The value circle contains deceptively simple truths about the interactions among stakeholders. One such truth is that companies don't have a *collection* of stakeholders; they have a *system* of stakeholders—there is a natural order to them all (Exhibit Two). This "system" surfaces

EXHIBIT TWO

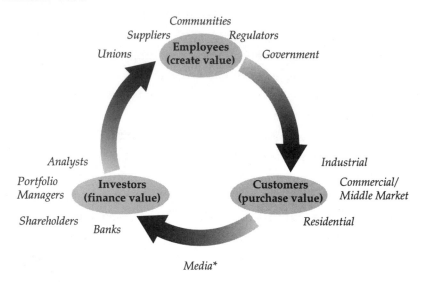

*Affect all stakeholders

in light of the economic interdependence that governs the relationship among employees, customers, and investors. It can be stated as follows:

- Everything begins with employees. *Employees create value* through their ideas and innovations, their talents, their experience and skills, and through the products and services they build, market, and sell, which are (or should be) proxies for the identities of their organizations.

- *Customers purchase value* to the extent that they like the offerings— that is, the value—they see. At stake are sales, revenues, and profits.

- In turn, *investors finance value*. Depending on whether they "approve of" the earnings that flow from the value "purchased" by customers, they put capital back into the organization. This act closes the loop on the value circle, fueling its momentum, ad infinitum.

But there is more to these relationships than pure economic inter-dependence. The credo that explains how the laws of identity shape our lives states that *"we most need those who need us in return."* From this perspective, employees *need* customers to affirm their worth as one enterprise—the things they are and do as one "team." It is as much a matter of pride and purpose as it is about a paycheck. Customers *need* employees to improve their lives through better products and services. Investors *need* employees, for they are the wellspring of ongoing earnings growth.

It is this model of value creation that was lacking in the speech about greatness delivered by senior Westinghouse executives in 1987. As a result, the speech foretold the end, not the beginning, of a great company. I will never forget the look of near defeat on the face of my day-to-day contact as we talked about how greatness comes to pass—that it can be achieved only by abiding by the logic of the value circle. As one Westinghouse manager said to me, being great meant investing, above all, in the relationship between employees and customers. "If we did that right," he allowed, "it just might produce the greatness management was looking for."

Another truth contained in the Law of Relationship, and revealed through the value circle, is that no one stakeholder group is more important than any other. It may be fashionable to talk about the primacy of investors, but it is foolhardy to operate accordingly. To do so usually means maximizing near-term profits, which can rob the company of vital growth capital. Selling out the future for the sake of the present is to *dis*invest in identity and ultimately to weaken the enterprise. In the final analysis, investors are best served by seeing themselves as the *beneficiaries* of the value created through the interaction between employees and customers.

The challenge to management is to maximize the productivity of the circle by keeping the interests of all principal stakeholders in balance. Smart employees need to appreciate the crucial role of investors; smart investors need to appreciate—and consciously invest in—the critical role of employees. Both need to recognize their particular relationship to customers. Westinghouse didn't play by these rules, and it was undone as a result. Upjohn erred on the side of employees by bowing to social priorities and was unable to sustain itself as an independent enterprise.

The value circle not only orders relationships among employees, customers, and investors; it also aligns other constituencies around the value creation process. For instance, suppliers are best positioned close to employees, for they have a direct effect on *creating* value through the parts, equipment, and credit terms they provide. The same goes for unions and government officials, both of whom influence the company's ability to create value—the former through their effect on wages, benefits, and other standards, the latter through regulation and legislation.

In this same vein, it is easy to see how segmenting customers and investors into their component parts leads to a deeper appreciation for the role each of these segments plays in the value creation process. What I have found to be most exhilarating is working with managers as they develop strategies and tactics for shaping these relationships to benefit their organizations.

It wasn't long after my engagements with Westinghouse that I realized that what energized the value circle—what gave it vitality—was putting a company's identity squarely at its center. In its own right, the value circle was a powerful tool for planning and implementation. But it took on far greater meaning for clients once they saw themselves within it. Alcoa's genius for transformation, AIS's passion for the science of industry, Korn/Ferry's need to build leadership capital—these were the centers of gravity that made the value circle come to life.

With identity at its center, the value circle inspires us to ask a crucial question: *Who must understand the identity of the company? Who must know what drives the corporate being?* The answer isn't obvious; it isn't, first and foremost, the customer. It is, rather, the employees, because they constitute the physical, mental, and emotional fabric of identity. They must know who, in the collective sense, they are—what they "add up to" as one enterprise. And then they must live accordingly.

The next most important group includes suppliers and others (such as unions) who have a direct effect on the value creation process. Why? Because their own corporate identities, as channeled through products, services, and policies, contribute to the robustness of the identity of the companies they do business with. As expressed through its identity, the unique characteristics of Delphi, for instance, one of the world's leading automotive suppliers, has a significant impact on Ford's ability to create value in the form of cars and trucks. The same can be said of the potent institutional identity of the United Auto Workers and its influence on value creation at Ford as well as at other car and truck manufacturers.

Another primary audience who must understand an organization's identity is its investors. Investors, particularly shareholders, money managers, and financial analysts, need to see what, or rather *whom*, they are actually investing in, and what the business and economic implications of this investment are. In my work with Upjohn, for example, the millions of dollars in incremental revenue that flowed from such "concept formulations" as panic disorder suggested the economic potential of the company's need to restore and maintain the integrity of human life. Similarly, Alcoa's aborted efforts to diversify around materials science held substantial promise for unleashing its genius for transformation as an engine for growth.

The situation with customers is different. In my experience, customers need most above all to see evidence of identity in all aspects of their relationship with an organization. This evidence comes in many forms: in the products and services they buy, in the return policies and warranties that measure the company's confidence in its offerings and itself, in the sense of belonging that customers ultimately feel in doing business with the company. For customers, *experiencing* the identity of an organization is far more important than their ability to articulate it.

The main task in working within the value circle is to help companies build a *relationship advantage* with all stakeholders by aligning their diverse interests through identity. The Law of Relationship makes the wisdom of completing this task clear: *Organizations are inherently relational, and those relationships are only as strong as the natural alignment between the identities of the participants.* "Participants" in this instance include all the stakeholders who determine the ability of the corporate being to thrive.

The payoff from operating within the context of the value circle is to maximize the number of people who "work for" the company—that is, to get more customers to buy more products and, in turn, deliver more revenue; to get suppliers to agree to better credit terms, allowing for better cash flow; to get employees to innovate around identity constantly, discovering new ways to deepen the roots of competitive differentiation; to get investors to keep their money with the company longer, thus reducing portfolio turnover and providing greater financial flexibility; and to get communities, figuratively speaking, to issue a "license to operate." Building a relationship advantage through the value circle makes a company more efficient on a grand scale.

When it comes to relationships, few organizations have ties to customers, and to society generally, that are as do-or-die important as the ties of utilities to these constituencies. New York State Electric & Gas (NYSEG) became my client in the fall of 1995. In the two years that I worked with NYSEG, I came to understand, more clearly than ever before, how the Law of Relationship determines success and failure. In many ways, the story of NYSEG is the story of how one utility bucked tradition and began to establish relationships on the basis of how it created value, rather than how it created energy.

NEW YORK STATE ELECTRIC & GAS

A Moment at Kirkwood

The meeting room in the Kirkwood facility in Binghamton, New York, headquarters for NYSEG, was simple and unadorned. It had no art on the walls, no distractions, only the screen at the front of the room and a long table, perhaps twenty by eight feet, that became at once a field of battle and a field of dreams.

Around the table sat various members of NYSEG's operating committee and a few high-ranking staff executives from legal, marketing, communications, and human resources—maybe fifteen people in all. The agenda was set. I was presenting, in summary form, my findings and my conclusions about how the company should position itself in the face of deregulation and open-market competition. Copies of the report had been distributed to the group in advance so that people would have time to consider its contents and be able to take part in a more meaningful discussion. The punch line of my presentation suggested that NYSEG wasn't just in the energy business; the company had a relationship with customers that was rich and complex and was destined to become more so.

Before the meeting I was coached by my primary client contact, Rita Saunders, manager of corporate communications, to encourage the group to ask questions. Rita wanted to make sure that the session was "interactive"; she wanted people to open up, to express their views. As it turned out, no such encouragement was needed. Judging by their reactions, everyone had obviously already read the material.

As soon as my presentation ended, the room came to life with an energy all its own. Slowly at first, and with rehearsed calm, a handful of managers let it be known that in their eyes, what I was describing had nothing to do with "the reality of the marketplace." In the face of competition, they explained, the energy business was primarily about two main things: first, the cost of supply (of electricity or natural gas) and NYSEG's resultant ability to provide customers with competitively priced energy, and second, top-notch service, including efficient billing systems and the ability to restore power quickly if it were interrupted.

It was no secret: The utilities industry was in the throes of monumental change. Regulated electric companies, independent power producers, nonutility generators and natural gas companies, regionally and nationally, were preparing for competition. Protected customer monopolies were about to become a thing of the past.

Everyone listened to the people who had the floor, and many heads nodded in agreement. But not all. In the quiet aftermath of these carefully worded comments, one of NYSEG's most senior officers leaned forward and offered a different view. He looked straight at the individual who had talked the loudest and said that the positioning of NYSEG that I had proposed was really the only way to go, adding that in the next several years, neither they nor any other utility would have much choice. *"It's going to be a different world."*

Like so many metal pellets falling under the spell of two opposing magnetic poles, I watched as the executives in the room migrated into two separate camps. One camp was willing to consider the possibility of a new world that mirrored my recommendation. The other was quite certain of the staying power of the one that currently existed. A clear line had been drawn between the two groups. It was a line that was predicated on ideology rather than simply economics. Everyone in that room—in that moment in Kirkwood—wanted the same thing: for NYSEG to succeed, to grow and prosper in an environment of deregulation. But that is where agreement ended, at least for the moment.

New Rules

As utilities go, New York State Electric & Gas isn't a leader in any conventional sense of the word. It isn't the largest concern, or even one of the largest, in the northeast. It doesn't serve a major urban market such as New York City or Washington, D.C. It isn't among the most profitable energy companies around. It isn't known for being a trend-setting innovator like Enron or Duke Energy. Yet on the strength of its identity, NYSEG, in its own way, would turn out to be on the leading edge.

Below the calm, conservative exterior of this seemingly old-line utility there were hundreds, if not thousands, of people who cared deeply about the business they were in. Line workers, for example, expressed concern over the prospect of cutting back the free installation of new, residential electric service lines from several hundred feet to far less. They wondered just how some customers would pay for the difference, given their very modest means.

Call center managers and employees dealt routinely with every kind of issue—from customers who wanted NYSEG to "forgive" late payments to those who were waiting for the newest energy management systems for their homes or offices. Some of the engineers I spoke with were quick to emphasize the "public trust" nature of their business and the twenty-four-hour-a-day procedures designed to make sure that there were no service interruptions. The deeper I went into the organization, the more I found a professional, at times even passionate, work force—the flesh and blood of NYSEG's identity.

My assignment was to help NYSEG's management develop a brand strategy that would become a cornerstone of the company's new marketing thrust, a platform for building competitive advantage in the company's south central New York State service territory and beyond. As it was stated in public documents, NYSEG needed to "manage a profitable transition to a market-based environment . . . to succeed in the energy-related businesses of the future. . . ." NYSEG would now have to compete in order to survive. No matter how it was stated, this 140-year-old company had to define and establish new relationships with a host of constituencies.

To deliver the brand strategy that had been asked for, I needed to go through a standard analytical process. This included a series of interviews with strategically important industrial and commercial customers—companies such as Corning and IBM, without whom NYSEG might not survive. To a person, the individuals who spoke for these organizations welcomed the prospect of "choice"; in the wake of deregulation, they would be able to pick the company from whom they purchased their electricity or natural gas. The idea of lower energy rates was tantalizing.

The same situation existed for all customers around the country, but it was especially appealing to NYSEG's customers because NYSEG's electricity prices were among the highest in the nation. The company was burdened by "stranded costs"—sunk costs associated with now-defunct nuclear plants—that were baked into the price of electricity. The concern also paid one of the highest tax rates in the United States.

In the course of my interviews, I found that despite the pent-up demand for lower rates, customers were also looking for more. Once customers had vented their frustration over price, they began to talk about other things: about wanting NYSEG to communicate with them more often, to get to know them better, to let them know "what was coming down the pike," and to tailor programs to meet their individual needs. For all the attention being paid to electric rates, almost equal (if less vocal) attention was being given to the human side of these relationships. I couldn't help but wonder whether a better relationship— more interaction, more focus on meeting customers' needs, more face-to-face contact, a fresh look at how energy and energy management might help solve business problems—might mitigate some of the frustration that surrounded the cost of the commodity itself.

NYSEG's other customer base, which consisted of its residential customers, was the company's principal source of revenue—and a notably different story. I found NYSEG's residential customers largely uninformed about deregulation. They were cynical as well. Their experience with telephone companies, since deregulation in the mid-1980s, had bred a certain amount of confusion and skepticism about the supposed benefits of competition. Some consumers spoke of "misleading or phony options" where switching from one carrier to another didn't produce the promised results. Like their industrial and commercial counterparts, however, they were more than ready to consider alternative energy providers offering lower prices. Listening closely, I sensed that consumers held NYSEG in genuine regard; the company had demonstrated consistent reliability in restoring power after it was lost and had contributed much to the community for over a century. At the same time, customers fumed over their fate at the hands of "a high-priced monopoly."

It was a time of unseen ironies at NYSEG, as I believe it was for numerous utilities at the threshold of open-market competition. Just as customers were beginning to feel a new sense of freedom and empowerment, many managers were talking about wanting to "own" the customer relationship. They were referring to the different ways in which NYSEG might create value for customers in the wake of deregulation, from selling them their fuel, to providing dependable service, to supplying an ever-widening array of value-added energy products and services for the office, the plant, or the home.

I realized that NYSEG's relationship with its customers was going to be governed by new rules. Certainly, price was going to be a material component of these rules, but price alone wouldn't be enough. To reach (to say nothing of "owning") the customer, NYSEG would have to learn to be at home in territory that had been largely foreign to it. It was the territory of true relationships, a high visibility landscape where value was defined by emotional as well as physical and intellectual terrain.

Unearthing the Meaning of NYSEG

My experience in cracking the code on identity has taught me that the only thing one can assume with complete confidence is surprise. It is impossible to know what you will ultimately discover. The corollary to this fact is that if you think you have the answer in advance, you are probably wrong.

The prospect of helping NYSEG position itself on the strength of its identity was especially intriguing to me. NYSEG was a company in an industry whose roots ran deep into the fabric of society. It was, like its brethren in utilities, an infrastructure business that made social and economic progress possible. The rhetorical question "Where would you be without us?" was, I thought, a perfect expression of their collective importance to us all.

As I began the identity analysis, the notion that NYSEG was merely the regional electric and gas company seemed far too simplistic, too pat. In terms of how NYSEG created value, there was more to this enterprise than met the eye—more than the enormous generation facilities, miles of transmission and distribution lines, and dozens of service trucks suggested. The urgent need I faced was to cut through the heavy underbrush that obscured the true value I knew lay beneath the surface of this company. It was a jungle of assumptions about price, delivery, and service being the *sine qua non* of differentiation.

Despite their obvious importance, I felt that none of these factors had anything to do with the fundamental identity of NYSEG. To accept them out of hand would have been to ignore an essential part of the sixth Law of Identity: *Relationships are only as strong as the natural alignment between the identities of the participants*. Nothing—not a competitive price, not timely and reliable delivery, not dependable service—is as important as this.

I realized that the only way to understand NYSEG's value creation process was to take a fresh, unencumbered look at the distinctive contribution the company made to its customers' lives and businesses. In a sense, I felt I needed to step back in time to see what the aggregate impact of energy had been over decades. A number of fundamental questions raced through my mind: What exactly were the benefits of this "miracle" called electricity and of other fuels, such as natural gas? What value had been hidden over time under the weight of regulation and the label of commodity? What opportunities existed to revitalize customer relationships once this value was revealed? These were the questions I needed to answer.

I set about deconstructing the company's value creation process one step at a time. In the course of my interviews, I asked executives, employees, and customers simple questions about the role energy plays in people's lives, what energy's inherent benefits were, and what it was that NYSEG did that allowed these benefits to surface. The pieces came together slowly. As they did, they told a story that held great promise for enhancing—and even for helping NYSEG eventually to "own"—the customer relationships it counted on.

At its most basic level, NYSEG's relationship with its customers was predicated on how the company helped people live and companies work. It was a relationship—or, more accurately, a bond—that virtually set to music the rhetorical question *Where would you be without us?* What quickly emerged from focus groups with residential customers was that people's health, their ability to eat safe, prepared food, their ability to travel, and their opportunity to be entertained and have fun were all tied to NYSEG's products and services. It didn't take long to spell out the business benefits of developing a deeper relationship with customers. The "benefits" weren't lower operating costs, however; they were productivity, safety, competitiveness, and growth—all of which, I found, had come to be to be taken for granted by as many managers as customers.

Although the benefits of doing business with NYSEG were now clear, the process of value creation—the connection between the company and its customers—still was not. Working from the benefits back upstream to the organization, I began to see what NYSEG actually did for customers. Basically, the organization enabled people to alter what amounted to the infrastructure of their own lives. Through NYSEG, for instance, individuals determined the climates of their homes and offices. They were able to see in spite of the dark, hear in the physical absence of others (radios), preserve and prepare food, and travel via public transit.

I saw that NYSEG's "gift" to its customers was the gift of control over basic elements: over air, light, sound, food, and movement. The facets of NYSEG's value creation process were fast falling into place. There was so much more than cheap energy and good service at stake. The notion that the company was strictly in a commodity business seemed ludicrous to me as the true nature of NYSEG's relationships with customers became clear.

Working with NYSEG as it sought to make a safe passage to the "other side" of regulation, I realized that time had been both its enemy and its ally. Over time, the public-trust role of this and other utilities had produced layers of regulation that only served to reinforce public perceptions of the company as a "commodity-producing monopoly." The essence of the organization's value had been lost in the process.

Over the same time, extraordinary technological advances had transformed how people worked and lived. All of these advances, and the human benefits they yielded, owed their existence to the utilities, which had provided the fuel that made it all possible. In making this connection, I finally understood the identity that drove this organization forward.

NYSEG was distinguished by a pervasive need to *help people shape their energy environments*—the initially raw spaces that, once converted, we know as homes, offices, and factories. In doing so, the enterprise improved the efficiency and quality of businesses and lives. The value creation loop was complete. NYSEG gave customers *control* over these environments, which, in turn, resulted in a host of personal and business benefits: *warmth, light, sound, and better food preparation; productivity, competitiveness, and growth* (Exhibit Three).

NYSEG's passion for shaping energy environments ran deep within the organization. Electric Generation's senior managers and rank-and-file engineers with whom I spoke obsessed over energy supply. Delivery executives went on about uninterrupted service and how to make service better "right up to the meter." Managers in the unregulated energy services business unit talked earnestly about their consulting relationships with customers and about "smart home" technology that would allow people to control climate and other aspects of their home environments better.

What I realized is that it took all of these operations to shape energy environments. I also realized that the identity of this institution provided the basis for shaping new relationships with customers.

Shortly after I had clarified NYSEG's identity and shared the results with the operating committee, the company appointed a new chief

EXHIBIT THREE

	Gives customers control over basic elements:	To affect:		And thus an abiltity to:	
	Air	→	Climate/Comfort/ Temperature	*Conduct Business*	*Live*
NYSEG helps shape the energy environment	Light	→	Ability to see	•Production	•Health
	Sound	→	Ability to hear	•Safety	•Eating
	Food	→	Preservation/ Preparation	•Competitiveness	•Travel
	Movement	→	Motion/ Transportation	•Growth	•Fun

executive, Wesley von Schack, former head of Duquesne Light in Pittsburgh. Over the years, I have found that new executives often put their stamp on a company by adopting a new mission or vision. It was an outcome I now feared—but one that never materialized. Soon after his appointment, Wes von Schack adopted the following articulation of NYSEG's identity as the company's vision: *"Helping companies and people shape energy environments that improve the efficiency and quality of their businesses and lives."* How NYSEG could compete and grow on the strength of this vision now weighed heavily on my mind. The challenge was no longer about discovery; it was about implementation.

Reshaping Relationships—The Process Begins

In the face of deregulation, one of NYSEG's top priorities was its relationship with its customers. Yet the company had numerous other constituencies to deal with as well, all of whom influenced its success. I knew that what my client needed to address all of its vital relationships was a comprehensive framework in which each stakeholder group had its rightful place, and where that place was clear to those at NYSEG who were on the front lines of managing these relationships.

Many opportunities to reshape relationships unfolded in the aftermath of Wes Von Schack's adopting identity as NYSEG's vision. The value circle was exactly what NYSEG needed to take advantage of these opportunities. What it provided NYSEG was *discipline*—a comprehen-

sive discipline for thinking and acting and for helping to turn vision
into reality.

Rita Saunders, my day-to-day contact at NYSEG, was a person of
great insight, skill, and vision. Although her title was manager of corporate communications, she saw the world, particularly the world of
NYSEG, from a multifaceted perspective. Rita was born with a passion
for "the brand" that enabled her to understand the value circle readily
and act effectively upon its logic.

Rita and I began to draw up plans and procedures for company-
wide implementation. One of the first things we needed to do was
change the messages the organization was sending in order to reinforce
its vision. This was, in the case of each constituency, a call for action
and a statement of how NYSEG intended to interact with that group.
Developing these messages was a first step in forging new relationships
that would benefit everyone involved. Here is an overview of the messages we prescribed for key constituencies:

To employees

*NYSEG is not just in the business of providing energy and good
service. . . . [W]e are—and always have been—in the business of
helping customers shape their energy environments in ways that
improve the efficiency and quality of their businesses and lives. Your
role, starting now, is to develop new means of doing so.*

To customers:

*NYSEG's job is to continually improve the efficiency and quality of
your businesses and lives by finding new ways to help you shape your
energy environment. . . . [T]o our business customers, we will focus on
boosting your productivity and competitiveness, we will aim to enhance
the safety of your workplace, and to contribute to your growth. To our
residential customers, individuals and families, we will use our skills
to contribute to your health, to the ease and reliability of transportation and to your ability to have fun.*

To investors:

*To drive its strategy for growth, NYSEG has defined its customers'
businesses and homes as distinct "energy environments," each having*

*its own particular characteristics and needs that NYSEG intends to
identify and meet. The goal, in meeting these needs, is to build the
company's brand franchise as the foundation for steady earnings
improvement.*

Taken together, these messages constituted the basis for forging a
new contract with NYSEG's most important stakeholders. They signaled the company's intent, new commitments on both sides of the
relationship equation, and the prospect of true alignment among these
vital constituencies.

The development and dissemination of these messages set the
stage for implementing changes that involved managers and employees across the company. One of the most compelling strategies we
crafted called for linking employees in every business unit with those
stakeholders with whom they had a direct, day-to-day relationship.
The aim was to marshal employees as channels to market in a way that
gently forged a more intimate relationship between NYSEG and its
constituencies.

Rita and I went through each business unit, identifying which
executives and employees had a primary relationship with each stakeholder group displayed around the value circle. We worked out who
was principally responsible for these relationships today, and then we
determined who *should* be involved, given their experience, knowledge, and day-to-day activities. The result was a matrix that illustrated
how NYSEG should ideally interact with its various constituencies. It
was a blueprint for operationalizing the value creation process from
the inside out (Exhibit Four).

Actual implementation called for training each group of employees. The "curricula" addressed their special roles as ambassadors of the
company, explained why they were selected, and outlined how this
role expanded the scope and importance of their jobs. The plan also
included coaching employees via "talking points" on what to say, for
instance, to the customers they dealt with, community officials, suppliers, government officials, and investors.

As with all implementations, we encountered a certain amount of
resistance. We met with skepticism on the part of several managers for

EXHIBIT FOUR

NYSEG – "Shaping Energy Environments"

	Primary Channels	Employees	Unions	Suppliers	Communities	Government	Regulators	Customers	Investors	Media
Executive	CEO									
	Executive vice president									
	CFO/CFO organization									
	Lines-of-business heads									
	Vice presidents									
Corporate	Corporate communication									
	Corporate planning/rates									
	Electric resource planning									
	Government affairs									
	Human resources									
	IBEW presidents									
	Purchasing									
	Shareholder services									
Lines of Business — Delivery	Call center									
	Consumer affairs									
	Consumer services managers									
	Economic development									
	Energy services									
	Engineering/O&C managers									
	Field employees									
	IBEW first-line supervisors									
	Managers/supervisors									
	Marketing and sales									
Genco	Managers/supervisors									
	Energy trading and power marketing									
	Plant managers									
Gas	Energy trading									
	Managers/supervisors									
External	Consumer advisory panel									

*Listed in alphabetical order.

whom this approach was foreign and who could not understand the reason for such broad-based employee involvement. In the course of conversation with some executives, I talked about the company's annual payroll investment. I pointed out that, possibly outside of major capital investment, there is no number as large as payroll that the company spends every year. I explained that the "return" on this investment needs to be measured and that the best way to do so is in terms of the value of the relationships the organization establishes with its stakeholders. Perhaps there wasn't complete agreement, but we at least succeeded in getting key executives to stop and consider the proposition and, in the end, allow the process to continue.

The Law of Relationship highlights the unseen connections among all the parts of an organization—its lines of business, its locations, its functions, even its products and services. It is in articulating these connections that the value of the whole is finally recognized to be greater than the sum of its parts. In NYSEG's case, the natural connection among all business units was brought to the fore through the lens of identity; the role each played in delivering on the promise of shaping energy environments was clear.

Customer Service and Energy Delivery was one business unit. To the public, it was the most visible part of NYSEG and thus, the main face and voice of the company. As such, the role we designated for it was to demonstrate NYSEG's commitment to helping people shape their energy environments through its daily interactions with customers.

Another business unit was Electric Generation, informally known as "Genco." Some Genco managers argued that shaping energy environments was solely an "after the meter" event—it took place *within* the home, factory, or office. Therefore, either generation had no place in the implementation plan, or the vision of the company was misguided.

I saw the situation differently. In my eyes, generation, or "supply," was central to shaping energy environments. After all, no supply meant no control over basic elements such as air, light, and sound. In this regard, Generation was at the very heart of NYSEG's identity. The specific role of this business unit also included reducing the cost of electricity as part of NYSEG's offering. In the larger scheme of things, Genco's job wasn't to reduce costs simply for the sake of staying competitive; it was to reduce costs in order to be better able to help people shape their energy environments.

Honing "the Team"

Spelling out these roles helped everyone understand where they fit into the bigger picture. But it also had another impact on NYSEG—an impact that goes to the heart of leadership for all organizations. Clarifying business unit roles in light of identity reveals managers who are resistant to change, resistant to operating in the best interests of the organization as a whole, rather than simply in the interests of their unit's profit and loss statement.

In almost every organization I have served, I have found an undercurrent of ambiguity, if not open disagreement, about what business the company "really is in," or about the relevance of the vision, or mission, to certain operating units and their managers. Such ambiguity, which is sometimes actively cultivated by a few managers, allows conflicts to simmer unresolved. In turn, these conflicts take their toll on productivity by undermining teamwork. Clarifying identity brings these conflicts to the surface. It reveals those people who don't agree with the articulation of identity, who don't like what they hear, or who simply want to be left alone to do their own thing.

I have witnessed fierce debates over conclusions about identity that shake up the status quo. Ironically, even in companies apparently in the throes of major change, where nothing is sacred, the agendas behind these "debates" are nearly always about *not changing*. Or they are about holding firm to existing definitions about what business the company is in (for example, NYSEG is in the energy business, period).

Identity removes ambiguity, painting a picture of the future that demands *corporation-wide* teamwork; no islands allowed. Identity-based management seeks efficiency on a grand scale. In light of identity, the adage "*Lead, follow or get out of the way*" takes on new meaning.

Six months into the process of implementation, Rita had managed to win the support of numerous managers who had exhibited varying degrees of doubt along the way. Many other initiatives were coming to life. Advertising was beginning to reflect NYSEG's vision ("Shaping Energy Environments" was being used as a tagline in many cases), as was the content of marketing and sales literature aimed at all three customer groups: industrial, commercial, and residential customers. The value circle itself became a tacit message that occasionally found its way into the fabric of communication.

As I watched the process unfold, I realized what was really taking place: NYSEG was starting to align itself with its own identity. If the process continued, I knew that the expected payoffs from building new relationships with stakeholders would eventually lead the organization to align what it said and what it did—how it conducted itself—with who it was. The result I envisioned was a relationship advantage for the company, where as many people as possible "worked for" NYSEG.

CULTIVATING INSTITUTIONAL ROOTS

Throughout this book, I often refer to companies as institutions. This isn't a casual description. The reason I use this term is best understood within the context of this sixth Law of Identity and, particularly, in light of NYSEG and other utilities. "Institution" is a word that, in its original meaning, acknowledges the relationship an organization has with the society, or culture, of which *it is necessarily a part*. No company has a choice in this matter. Whether the organization is large or small, there is a role for it to play, and value for it to create, that goes beyond the immediate customer.

Institutional relevance is a hallmark of many market leaders whose relationships with others, knowingly or not, appear to be founded on their identities: Johnson & Johnson, Disney, DuPont, Alcoa, Coca-Cola. They have all woven themselves inextricably into the fabric of our lives, shaping our expectations about how we will meet our most basic needs—for health, for fun, for comfort, for transportation, for refreshment. They are all fulfilling their *institutional* obligations as part of the value creation process—a process that produces wealth in return.

Developing institutional roots is a rite of passage for all companies aspiring to leadership. And it is a passage that often comes in the form of a crisis that rakes identity over the coals. Take Nike, the world leader in the athletic shoe business. The company's seemingly impenetrable "brand greatness" was rocked publicly in 1998 by fierce criticism of its manufacturing and wage scale practices in Asia.

What this produced was an *institutional imperative* for the enterprise. Nike had to *reattach* itself to the society it employed in ways that better met *that society's* demands. Their was no other course for the company to take, not if it hoped to maintain its franchise. Nike's trials illustrate yet another way in which the Law of Relationship governs business life. *Organizations are inherently relational, and those relationships are only as strong as the natural alignment between the identities of the participants.*

As institutions, utilities are a paradox. They are deeply relevant to a healthy, functioning society. Yet many utilities insist on basing their relationships with society almost exclusively on such mundane, though important, business factors as the price of electricity or gas and the reliability of their service in the wake of power outages. They have lost sight of the true value they create for us all—for businesses and individuals alike. They have stopped selling the most compelling features and benefits of what they have to offer.

Perhaps deregulation will force utilities to tell their stories better— to describe in more human and compelling ways what they really do, how they fit into society, and where we would be without them. If this is what is in store, then NYSEG is ahead of the game.

One of the challenges we all face in attempting to adhere to the Law of Relationship is trying to understand the identity of others—other individuals or other organizations. Under ideal circumstances, we can do this before the relationship is formed, or before it heats up, because genuinely knowing the identity of the other party is vital to the success of that relationship. Whether for love or money, the stakes are high. Aligning identities is the most effective way to ensure mutually rewarding, long-term relationships. But meeting this challenge of insight can be extremely difficult.

How can people, particularly those in leadership positions, come to know the identity of other organizations before the fact? Clearly, one cannot simply peer into the soul of another company and see what makes it tick. But it is possible to construct a telling picture that can foreshadow success or failure far better than what managers can discern by simply predicting economic outcomes. Constructing such a picture is a matter of decoding how a company creates value, not in terms of wealth for shareholders, but in terms of the benefits it delivers to customers and society. There is no organization whose identity cannot be discerned by deconstructing its value creation process.

Managers who embrace the sixth Law of Identity must attempt to understand all of their organization's primary external relationships in terms of what overarching need drives the other party. This holds for all stakeholders and particularly for customers, suppliers, and investors, without whom the organization simply cannot create value.

7 THE LAW OF COMPREHENSION

**THE INDIVIDUAL CAPACITIES OF AN
ORGANIZATION ARE ONLY AS VALUABLE
AS THE PERCEIVED VALUE OF THE WHOLE
OF THAT ORGANIZATION.**

I am alive, I am unique, and I am immutable,
even as I grow and evolve.
To truly live, however, I must express myself fully,
and in this regard, have much to give.
But to do so, I need others, and am most productive
with those who need me in return.
To establish these relationships, I must
first be recognized for who I am,
and it follows then that
I will receive in accordance with what I give.

One of the underlying themes of the Laws of Identity is that we must take responsibility for ourselves as individuals, and for "ourselves" as organizations—responsibility for building productive relationships, for pursuing our personal dreams and corporate aspirations, for our success, or for our lack of success if that is what transpires in the end. In a previous chapter, we saw how the Law of Possibility addresses this need directly. So does the Law of Comprehension. To "know thyself" is the essential beginning, but it is up to us to make sure that others, particularly those who matter to us, fully comprehend the unique characteristics that make us who we are and that are the foundation of how we create value.

The challenge of being recognized for who we are arises in many different ways, hundreds of times a day. For individuals, it occurs in the résumés we construct about ourselves, in the stories people tell about us, and in the reputations we develop in our work and with our friends and families. For business organizations, the Law of Comprehension sets up a challenge for managers in search of loyal customers, employees, investors, and others without whom their organizations would wither and die. It is the challenge of being known not simply for the company's products and services, but also for who the company is as an individual in its own right. Products and services and their features and benefits are tangible, concrete, "new and improved"—in relative terms, easy to sell. For this very reason, however, they constitute an ever-present, potentially dangerous distraction from corporate identity that must sometimes be avoided if the company is to be understood in its totality.

Ensuring that the identity of the organization is comprehended internally and externally is the responsibility of every leader, whether he or she is the CEO, a project team leader, or the head an elite corps of hard-charging sales representatives. It can be a tricky business. Not surprisingly, the need to increase revenues drives managers, and often their advertising agencies, to invest their time, creative energy, and budgets in selling products and services. Often the institution behind these offerings is seen as secondary in importance. (I recall a frustrated executive at German industrial giant BASF telling me how one of his more strident colleagues challenged him to explain how promoting BASF, the corporation, helped sell "even one more pound" of specialty chemicals.)

The CEO can never completely delegate the management responsibility implicit in the Law of Comprehension. He or she is the first steward of the identity of the enterprise. No one has a greater vested interest in making sure that all stakeholders understand the identity that explains *the value of the whole*. At the same time, top managers' success in this role is best measured by how well they have brought everyone into the fold. Do the people on the factory floor, in accounting, and in sales and marketing take seriously their personal role as part of the identity of the organization? Has their behavior evolved to the point where making *identity-based decisions* is second nature?

The seventh Law of Identity, the Law of Comprehension, demands more than the traditional marketing and communications functions to bring it fully to life. First and foremost, it is fueled by how employees speak of the company and how they behave during and after work. This law is further reinforced through the products and services that are (or should be) the natural expression of identity and through the policies and practices of the company toward the communities in which it lives. If the whole is to be recognized as greater than the sum of its parts, then the value of the whole must be visible in each of its parts. The same holds true for individuals. People we call leaders tend to be known for the totality of who they are, not simply for one or two skills. This applies to CEOs, managers, professionals, and employees at every level.

It is only in the last ten years or so that I have taken deliberate steps to be known for who I am. My ability to help companies understand themselves better—to point out strengths and opportunities camouflaged by products, organizational layers, and assumptions about what business they were in—led me to see, and finally to pro-mote, the value I create and the identity that is its bedrock.

In 1996 I left Anspach Grossman Portugal, which had gone through a major upheaval two years earlier. 1994 had been a year of turmoil. Founding partners had departed in the wake of a buyout by the WPP Group, and, a new CEO was ultimately brought in from the outside.

For the first time in sixteen years, I was faced with the need to take stock of myself and express my qualifications in the form of a résumé and letters. As foreign and difficult as this was to do, I found it exhila-rating. It gave me an opportunity to assess my achievements and artic-ulate who I was. I described my problem-solving experience and my role in AGP's business development efforts. I also took the opportunity to think through, and promote in conversations, the characteristics that defined me: among them, a passion for intellectual creativity and an ability to think in terms of whole-system solutions. It was an exer-cise that became a window not only on *what* I had done, but also on *who* I had become.

The results of letting people know exactly what I stood for were lib-erating. Almost immediately, I felt a greater sense of personal integrity—more honest, more complete, more confident. Professionally, I began to come in contact with other like-minded people. I started working with more clients who wanted what I had to offer in terms of a deeper, more comprehensive approach to identity consulting. Since that time, I have had the privilege of addressing a growing number of companies and business research organizations on this same subject.

One of the most dramatic organizational examples of the Law of Comprehension at work is Interbrew, the multi-billion-dollar, privately held, Belgium-based beverage concern that acquired Labatt of Canada in 1995. Interbrew came to be as the result of a merger in 1989 between Artois and Piedboeuf, two of Belgium's largest and most successful breweries. Artois was the company behind Stella Artois, one of the leading lager brands in Europe. Piedboeuf held the commanding market share in Belgium with its Jupiler brand. Both brought additional operations in mineral waters and soft drinks. Combined, the new company offered a collection of specialty beers that exceeded three hundred different brands. The story of Interbrew is a story of creation—the creation of an enterprise from the bottom up.

INTERBREW

Jupille Brewery, Spring 1990

Josie Renquin and I pulled up to the brewery just before 7 AM. Josie was a senior member of Interbrew's communications staff and my guide that morning. It was barely light as we worked our way through the pale yellow brick and glass entrance, across the rotunda-like entryway, past numerous faceless office doors, and back into the recesses of the plant where the focus group was to take place.

The room adjacent to the filling lines had been jerry-rigged with a makeshift table and chairs the night before, especially for this meeting. The lighting was poor; the smell of beer hung low in the room. We were met by a group of six men who appeared to range in age from their mid-twenties to their fifties. Nearly all were dressed in the same medium-blue overalls. The group and I watched each other intently as I took a seat across the table from them. As I looked into their faces, I could tell that they had little understanding of why we were there. Yet I sensed a willingness on their part to be good soldiers and to participate—after all, much was changing at this place now known as Interbrew.

Josie introduced me in French—no one in the group spoke English. I had worked hard the day before to simplify and translate into French a series of questions about how these individuals felt the merger would affect their lives and work. While I relied on Josie as my translator, I called upon my own limited French as a gesture of good faith.

The hour and a half that followed was at times awkward and cumbersome. I had to listen, digest, and reframe questions on the fly. About an hour into the meeting, one young man leaned over to another and whispered something inaudible. He then looked at me and Josie and began to talk more freely than anyone had so far.

His message was simple: To a man, these people were scared, but not about losing their jobs. They were scared of losing the *identités spéciales* that came with being part of Piedboeuf, the centuries-old organization that produced Jupiler, the best-selling beer in Belgium. They were afraid that there would be nothing left of the passion and dedication that they, their co-workers, and in some cases their families had brought to this company for so long—that it would all be swept away by the tidal wave of the merger.

As he spoke, the young man's colleagues nodded in vigorous agreement. Suddenly, the room became animated and alive with unspoken questions. With each passing moment, eyes were trained more intently upon me, as if to ask, "What will happen? What can we expect?" The truth is, I didn't know what to say. It was early in the assignment, and the challenge of discerning and then implementing identity in the wake of the merger had left many questions as yet unanswered.

As the session drew to a close, I considered how insignificant these workers must have felt in the overall scheme of things. As much as they may have been right on one hand—certainly, they couldn't influence investment decisions or the like—they were wrong in believing they were not important. In my eyes, each of these individuals was a vital cell in the overall genetic makeup of this nascent corporate being. And in this respect, I thought, each would be critical to the composition and forward momentum of the whole. If Interbrew was to succeed, then these workers and thousands of others like them would need to be part of the solution; they would need to be engaged in bringing this organization to life. The question was how.

A "Need for Identity"

As CEO of Interbrew, José Dedeurwaerder was a man of strong convictions; he was driven in the best sense of the word. This trait was evident as we spoke over lunch at the Four Seasons restaurant in New York, shortly after the assignment began in February 1990. With electricity in his eyes, José talked passionately about Interbrew's need for identity. It wouldn't be enough, he allowed, to have a good strategy and to "finesse" the economics and structure of integration. If Interbrew was to succeed, it would have to have, and live, an identity all its own. To his everlasting credit, Jose understood that the human side of the new enterprise needed as much attention as its purely economic side.

José had made his point: *Don't just change names, logotypes, and mission statements; change the way employees live and work.* The identity consulting he sought was not a matter of *designing* the "corporate house"; it was the entire process of building it from the ground up—to as close to the point of completion as possible.

Working with The Boston Consulting Group, José and his executive team resolved to create, on the strength of the merger, an international beverage company whose combined brand-reach extended well beyond the borders of Belgium. Aggressive growth was the goal. The removal of onerous trade barriers across Europe, in 1992, was just around the corner. Management wanted to position Interbrew to take advantage of this sea change and, eventually, to establish beachheads in Asia and North America.

As José and I discussed it, the identity assignment was framed by three needs. The first was to blend Artois and Piedboeuf, along with new "outside" managers, into one organization. The second was to commence Interbrew's assimilation into the international business arena. The third was to develop a marketing-driven enterprise in place of one that was heavily production-driven. What was left unsaid was the most important need of all. In fact, it was the need that, once met, would allow the others to be satisfied in turn: that need was to discern exactly what it meant to be "Interbrew." It was clear to me that Artois and Piedbouef were two distinct beings. It was a foregone conclusion that each company possessed its own unique characteristics; what these were, I needed to discover.

As I started the analysis, I wrestled with how I would get at the sum of the parts in a way that revealed a new and viable whole. I realized that the best way to discern Interbrew's identity would be to operate from the outset as though Artois and Piedbouef *were already one company*. It would then be a matter of articulating the potential that resided within that organization.

Mergers challenge the sanctity of identity. By definition, if not by design, they tear at the fabric of organizations by demanding change that threatens their unique value-creating characteristics. And yet, the need for people to "comprehend" these characteristics in the newly merged entity is paramount and immediate. Customer relationships are often being materially reshaped, like it or not. The continued avail- ability of investor capital in the form of equity is at stake. Employees can be traumatized by their fear of the unknown, a fear that can under- mine their productivity. With these thoughts uppermost in my mind, I struggled to think of a model that made sense to me—one that sug- gested the possibility of long-term success rather than failure.

Early one morning, at about 3 A.M. in my hotel room in Brussels, I was unable to sleep and decided to call home. It was 9 P.M. in Connecticut, so I knew I wouldn't be waking anyone up. After about a ten-minute conversation with my wife, I said good night and returned to bed. As I was falling asleep, I realized that the best model for under- standing identity within the context of mergers was *the family*. I thought about how all the members of my family were different, unique in their own right, and yet how, as a unit, we formed an iden- tity that was distinct to the family itself. I further considered how our family was initially formed—that is, through the mutual attraction Jan and I had for one another—and how our identities had been "naturally aligned" from the start as the basis for building our relationship.

As I pondered this analogy, I realized that the objective in the case of Interbrew was not to create a family in the literal sense. (To do so in business can lead to what a manager once described to me as "forgive- ness to a fault.") But the model, I thought, was still logical, for it called directly upon many of the Laws of Identity that collectively govern the lives and fortunes of organizations and individuals alike.

A Fragile Time

Interbrew's strategy for aggressive growth shook the foundation of both cultures. It put the organization on an unfamiliar course that served as a wake-up call to many people. One long-time executive described the merger as tough and uncomfortable. The "struggle to know what we are becoming" was a theme I heard a hundred times in as many different ways over the course of the engagement.

The question of what business Interbrew was in was the immediate issue. The Boston Consulting Group had pushed hard on the view that Interbrew was a *beverage* company—that it needed to build on its beers heritage, while at the same time developing and extending its growing strength in waters and soft drinks. Managers and employees weren't so sure. Many of them clung fast to the notion that Interbrew was essentially "a beer company" and that to say otherwise was misleading. Other views surfaced. One senior executive, a new manager from outside the ranks of either Artois or Piedboeuf, saw Interbrew as being a four-pronged portfolio business that included lager beers, specialty beers, waters, and soft drinks.

As people debated the "what business are we in" issue, I set about deconstructing the respective cultures of Artois and Piedboeuf. It was only a starting point, but it was important to begin to understand the psychology of each company in order to gauge how easy, or difficult, it was going to be to effect a true merger.

It took me only a short time to see how starkly different these organizations were. As I conducted my interviews, I quickly learned that Artois and Piedboeuf were "like Coke and Pepsi." The rivalry between them contained its own passion that had had little to do with their competing flagship brands, Artois's Stella Artois and Piedboeuf's Jupiler. It was a rivalry born of different heritages.

Artois was Flemish, the area of Belgium known for its industrious business orientation, whereas Piedboeuf was French. Artois was open, more extroverted, more communicative, even somewhat patrician. The company was more risk-oriented and more receptive to change. Its outlook was also more "international;" Stella Artois was one of the leading brands of beer in France and other markets outside Belgium.

Piedboeuf was more private and introverted. Despite Jupiler's status as the number-one beer in Belgium, its culture was viewed as less business-savvy. It kept a lower profile than Artois and was less inclined to open communication. Moreover, the organization struck me as more regimented in its management style and less likely to embrace risk as a part of doing business. Finally, Piedbouef was more provincial; its general focus was largely domestic, which came as no surprise, given Jupiler's commanding Belgian market share.

The harsh contrasts between these two founding companies brought into sharp relief the task that lay before me. The task was further complicated by the need to integrate into the fabric of Interbrew a group of outside senior managers who represented yet a third "culture." The collective experience of these executives—José Dedeurwaerder, the CEO, was one of them—reflected a non-beer perspective, a strong international outlook, sophisticated consumer marketing savvy, and a "big company" view. Their backgrounds included posts with Nestlé, Renault, and Philips NV.

For all the complexity that these various cultures represented, one thing was clear. There was no turning back; *Interbrew would be*. The journey that lay before the organization demanded significant changes. Now, as Interbrew, Artois and Piedboeuf would have to move from production-driven to being marketing-driven, from volume-oriented to more quality-oriented in all aspects of the business, from family shareholder–focused to consumer-focused, and from generally reactive to customer needs to proactive—especially as the first stage of European integration approached in 1992 and with it a new world of opportunities.

Interbrew Emerges

The overriding principle that governed my assessment of this just-formed organization was to treat it as though it had always simply been one being, alive in its own right, with a mind of its own. To do otherwise could easily lead me down the wrong path. In evaluating Artois's distinct strengths, for instance, I could wind up missing the crucial connective tissue that revealed how these two organizations created value now as one.

There was another potential distraction I needed to guard against. It would have been expedient for me to bow to the belief of some managers that it was the *products* that really mattered and that, accordingly, corporate identity wasn't something to worry about. But that didn't ring true for José and certainly not for me. Instinctively, José recognized the need for the organization to have its own identity. It was *Interbrew* that needed to be "sold" to trade customers—the retailers and "HORECA" owners (hotels, restaurants, and cafés) whom Interbrew relied on for distribution.

The plan also called for promoting Interbrew to consumers as a mark of quality. José understood that if employees didn't buy into the merger as the body, mind, and soul of Interbrew, the product brands that these people so cherished, and were responsible for creating and nurturing, would ultimately suffer.

I focused on discerning what strengths underscored this company's ability to create value—to make a proprietary contribution in its expanding marketplace. What I discovered were five specific capacities that very much belonged to Interbrew as a whole. The first was Interbrew's *capacity to endure*. Both founding organizations had long histories. Artois's roots stretched back to 1366, giving Interbrew a heritage that included over six hundred years of experience in brewing, selling, and serving one of Europe's prominent beers, Stella Artois.

The second strength I identified was Interbrew's *capacity for managing the art and science of occasions*. For all its knowledge of brewing and distribution, it was this aspect of its growing beverage competence that held the key to how Interbrew created value. In its more than six hundred years of life, this organization had come to understand how to capitalize on the moments in people's lives when beverages helped make an occasion meaningful and memorable. Such "moments" were pervasive. They included times when meals were taken, when holidays and anniversaries were celebrated, when parties were held, or simply when people got together. As Interbrew's strength in this area became clear, I sensed uptapped potential: Why not market *Christmas* beers or other special-occasion brands? And if existing products didn't work, then why not develop new ones? The importance of this particular capacity could not be underestimated. Inherent in each of these occasions, no matter how large or small, were the seeds of ever-greater consumption. And knowing exactly how Interbrew's products related to every such occasion was the key to growth for the company.

Interbrew's third capacity was its *capacity for leadership*. This aptitude was most clearly evident on two fronts. First, it came through in Stella Artois's unique heritage and product pedigree. If Interbrew had an international brand, this was it. The brand had survived centuries of change, and although it had had its economic ups and downs, it had established a loyal and growing following. Interbrew's other claim to leadership came in the form of Jupiler's dominant domestic market share. Although it was not so glamorous or well known as Artois, Jupiler's track record was superior in terms of overall economic performance. It was simply, in the eyes of many managers and employees, "Belgium's best beer."

The fourth strength was Interbrew's *capacity for product diversity coupled with deep specialization*. Few companies could claim to offer the range of beverage brands that Interbrew offered. Taken together, these brands met virtually every taste. To drive its growth strategy, management had organized the company around three product classes: Pils and lagers, waters and soft drinks, and specialty beers. Each of these classes not only embodied its own business psychology and personality but also, as I began to see, represented its own way of life.

Pils/lagers was about mass appeal and quantity. These products constituted a "social escape"; the experience of consuming them was steadfastly predictable. The "waters and softs," as they were called, appealed to people's desire for fitness, health, and freshness. But it was the specialty beers that had contained the greatest potential for distinguishing Interbrew. Interbrew's three hundred specialty beer brands ranged from "white" beers such as Hoegaarden to flavored beers such as those reminiscent of cherries or raspberries. This product class was a world unto its own that revealed the company's capacity for specialization—a world founded upon craftsmanship and exclusivity that appealed to esoteric, idiosyncratic tastes.

Interbrew's fifth capacity for value creation was its *capacity for human influence—how individuals live their lives*. For instance, Interbrew's specialty beers were its gift to the individualistic nature of all people. Taken together, Interbrew's beverage portfolio was a mirror of the full range of people's passions and aspirations. It reflected moments of victory and defeat, of pleasure and fantasy, of health and relaxation—the full gamut of human expression and experience.

I weighed these five capacities. What did they represent in the aggregate? Neither Artois nor Piedbouef, separately, could have laid claim to all these particular strengths. But together, these capacities formed the organization's five pillars of value creation. How exactly *did* Interbrew create value? I felt that these individual strengths held the seeds of the company's formative identity and, as such, had the potential to galvanize the organization into one productive being.

Late in the spring, some three months after the assignment began, I was sitting in the office of the corporate secretary, reviewing some of the findings that had emerged. As I sat there, three facts kept running through my mind. The first was that Interbrew seemed committed to beverages, not just beers. The second was that the organization, almost to a person and despite inherent rivalries between founding companies, was wholly dedicated to satisfying consumers and their diverse tastes. The third was that everyone—from top management to the production workers I had met with in Jupille two months earlier—had a profound desire to "survive the merger and succeed."

As I was listening to the corporate secretary, the pieces suddenly came together: Interbrew was driven by a need to *celebrate people's thirst for life*. It was a statement of fact, a pervasive ambition that distinguished the company and set the tone, the ground rules, and the challenge for achieving success as an international beverage concern.

As I let this idea sink in, I reviewed the composition of the enterprise. Interbrew's need to celebrate a thirst for life at once transcended and embraced the company's diverse lines of business and vast portfolio of brands. In fact, each business contributed to and shared the company's identity, despite the different economic and operating realities that set one business apart from the others and despite different brand "personalities" that matched different consumer lifestyles.

Interbrew certainly was in the business of satisfying thirsts, but its innate drive to celebrate a thirst for life spoke to more; it acknowledged what I had come to see as the employees' desire to continue to be the best in their field. Interbrew's identity was the life force behind a merger that was destined to succeed. I now needed to define precisely what Interbrew's thirst for life meant and then find ways to encourage its practice in the organization's day-to-day activities. As

José had said, the task was as much about identity implementation as about discovery.

From Identity to Culture

The power of identity to help make the merger work came from two things: the fact that it reflected the experience, aspirations, and personal values of the employees themselves and the fact that it was built upon distinct capacities that, together, drove company performance.

Like many just-merged companies, however, Interbrew was in danger of becoming no more than a holding company for its business units and brands. The longer employees saw themselves as part of either of the two original companies, the greater the chances that Interbrew would ossify, remaining neither fish nor fowl, and that the organization would never achieve its potential. Interbrew's managers and employees needed a framework that made sense for integration as well as change. As I found in the course of my interviews, they were looking for "values" that would help guide behavior on their journey toward becoming a truly international, consumer-driven enterprise.

Identity gives rise to culture. It was a lesson I had learned years earlier in my work with Alcoa and Fidelity. I would never forget it, for it was a lesson that came directly from the first two Laws of Identity, the Law of Being and the Law of Individuality. As I recalled this fact, I realized that certain values were inherent in Interbrew's identity—and that to celebrate a thirst for life, this organization would have to behave in ways that allowed it to create value accordingly. To live its identity, however, the company had to be drawn out of its shell. Interbrew needed to see itself from the outside in, as well as from the inside out. For all of their combined strengths, Artois and Piedboeuf were too parochial.

To get people to look beyond the boundaries of Belgium, and even of Europe, and in turn to speed the process of internationalization, I decided to take an outside-in approach. I decided to review the operating principles of four leading, global companies. Each was a potential role model for Interbrew that offered the organization a fresh perspective on the challenges it faced. Two of them were in the beer and beverage business, but two I chose deliberately because they were not. Interbrew, I believed, needed to see itself as a marketing company, not just a beverage company. The organization needed to be shaken up—in some ways even more than the merger had done.

The first company I looked at was Anheuser-Busch, the world's largest brewing enterprise. It had a rich American heritage. But most important for Interbrew, it had a pioneering tradition with values to match. The second company was Coca-Cola. It was the epitome of the American free-enterprise system and marketer of the world's most famous and ubiquitous brand. Using Coke as a role model would send a powerful message to Interbrew about how world-class brand management worked.

The third role model was Procter & Gamble. This classic consumer products company had written the book on marketing packaged goods. For Interbrew, P&G could demonstrate the overarching importance of knowing the consumer, above all, as the foundation for business success. The last role model I presented to Interbrew was Apple Computer. Apple was an iconoclast from the start and, by the early 1990s, stood for anti-establishment entrepreneurs come of age. Apple had changed the world through computers—I felt that Interbrew aimed to "change the world" through its need to celebrate its thirst for life.

From my analysis of these benchmark companies, I selected six values that were most appropriate for Interbrew and that aligned naturally with the organization's identity.

- *Putting the consumer first.* The people who drank Interbrew's beverages were the company's "best friends." Putting the consumer first in everything the company did was the only path to success.

- *A craftsman-like dedication to quality.* Quality was a matter of pride as well as profits. It was a statement of who the organization was and how much employees valued their business as a whole. Dedication to quality wasn't just a set of standards for making and selling beverages; it was a way of life that embraces all aspects of Interbrew.

- *The constant pursuit of professionalism.* Through their professionalism, employees contributed to the reputation of the company. This came to life in people's words, attitudes, actions, and appearance and through the wisdom they showed in the decisions they made every day on behalf of the organization.

- *A passion for communication.* Communication was the bridge between vision and reality, between one department and another, between the company and the customer, and among all individuals, regardless of their status, responsibilities, or experience.

- *An unshakable reliance on teamwork.* Taking a vigorous approach to teamwork was the only way to capitalize on the diverse skills, talents, and experience within the organization. Teamwork was a way of working, learning, getting to know one another, and performing as one enterprise.

- *A hunger for innovation.* Innovation would keep Interbrew fresh and vibrant. It was essential for leadership. As it resulted in better products for consumers, innovation would also lead to better relations with trade customers and to a constantly challenging environment to work in.

On the Road to Change

The Law of Comprehension speaks to one's need to see something in its entirety, to feel it, to experience it—ultimately to "get it." If employees were going to "get" and live what it meant to be Interbrew—to celebrate people's thirst for life—they needed to be able to grasp the true nature of the company in simple, compelling ways. They needed to see themselves as a vital part of the organization and to include Interbrew as an integral part of their own lives.

Where the Law of Relationship supplies a *framework* for implementation through the value circle, the Law of Comprehension reveals the *tools* of implementation, tools for building the enterprise around its identity. How I discovered those tools and then applied them illustrates the intimate connection between human identity and corporate identity. Like so many things, this connection reaffirms the need first to "know thyself."

Over the course of the two years I spent with Interbrew, I often used the office of Jacques Tibault as a temporary workplace. Jacques was director of training and development for Interbrew. It was there, on a sunny afternoon, that one of my colleagues and I unraveled the mystery of how to get thousands of employees to begin the process of change.

For all the books I had read concerning change, I felt that the only way to get at the answers I needed was to figure it out for myself, not intellectually but emotionally. What, I wondered, would get *me* to change if *I* were in these people's shoes—if I harbored their doubts, and if I wanted to succeed but wasn't certain of the future?

As I sat in Jacques's quiet office that afternoon, I imagined myself as one of these individuals. In the minutes that followed, I *felt* my way through the process of change, experiencing and recording, in my mind, what would actually work and what wouldn't. What I discovered first was that I wanted to be *involved* in some concrete way, not simply to be told what to do. I also realized that I needed to be guided; I was looking for a frame of reference that was logical as well as personal. Finally, I knew that if I were being totally honest with myself, I would have no choice but to change if I wanted to continue to belong. Although I do not believe that this analysis yielded a process that is universally applicable, I do believe that it supplied reliable insights into how Interbrew should move ahead. If these were the criteria for success, then what were the steps needed to implement them?

The following months were devoted to conducting dozens of cross-functional employee focus groups designed to translate Interbrew's identity-based values into action. All divisions and all levels of the company were part of the process. If there was an underlying aim, it was to get the organization to solve its own problem, to figure out for itself what it meant to celebrate a thirst for life.

Each group was asked the same basic question and given the same charter. The question was "How would your job change tomorrow morning if Interbrew were truly living according to the values of putting the customer first, making quality a way of life, and practicing teamwork regularly?" I imposed only two conditions: Don't concern yourself with what it might cost to effect the change, and ignore the politics that might attend your ideas. Although these issues might indeed arise and require attention, it was vital at this stage that people speak their minds freely, without regard to such considerations.

What transpired was nothing less than the liberation of the organization in the form of knowledge and know-how that had lain dormant until now. The painstaking process of conducting these groups and analyzing the results revealed hundreds of behaviors that painted a rich and varied picture of exactly what it meant to *celebrate a thirst for life* at the most basic operating level.

The actions taken as an outgrowth of these groups were in many cases mundane. For instance, professionalism meant making point-of-sale site visits mandatory for all international managers, preparing in advance for customer visits, and establishing a basic dress code for the sales force. This was where the roots of human productivity were to be found—in the thousands of things people did every day.

As I pondered these results, I realized that the values themselves were by no means unique to Interbrew; many companies subscribed to "putting the consumer first," "a commitment to quality," and the like. What *was* unique was how these values were *interpreted* by these particular individuals. I realized that it is through this process of interpretation that true differentiation occurs and that the success of even the grandest strategy hinges on the day-to-day conduct of employees.

Making sense of the results in their entirety was a challenge in its own right. What I found was that the behaviors associated with each particular value illuminated the overall *structure and content* of that value (Exhibit Five). The structure came through in the specific *dimensions* that framed each value and suggested where it most needed to be practiced. For instance, *putting the consumer first* came to life in the context of three particular areas: respect and responsiveness, consumer education, and public policy.

"Consumer-first" behaviors also implied the *beliefs*, or attitudes, employees needed to adopt in order to live that value. "Making it easy

EXHIBIT FIVE

Dimensions	Respect and Responsiveness	Education	Public Policy
Philosophies	• Make it easy on the consumer. • Anticipate, don't react. • Honesty is the best policy. • Marketing is the bridge to the consumer/ Everyone is a marketing person at Interbrew.	• All employees are ambassadors of Interbrew. • An educated consumer is the best customer.	• Protect the consumer. • A green, clean environment makes business sense. • Health-conscious consumers are valuable customers.
Actions	• Create a consumer-driven organization chart. Put the consumer on top; customers next; management on the bottom. • Establish a centralized consumer center to 1) answer complaints immediately and 2) route consumer feedback to the appropriate group(s). • Make all communications to consumers absolutely clear in terms of key benefits and language. • Provide detailed information on labels. Specify ingredients, print sale dates clearly, and ensure labels are legible. • Add toll-free number and company address to products to stimulate consumer feedback. • Avoid disinformation or misleading advertising (e.g., be realistic in communicating low chances of winning sweepstakes promotions). • Never run out of stock at point of sale. • Develop/promote "screw-off" bottle cap technology. • Make a science of understanding occasions and purchase dynamics. • Make market research the "consumer's voice" for the whole corporation.	• Distribute a sample collection of products to every new employee. Encourage employees to "sell" Interbrew to friends. • All new employees must get tours of all plants. • Give booklet on brand histories and corporate history to all employees. • Seat Interbrew as the authority and rightful educator on the world's beers.	• Avoid product risks. • Actively promote Interbrew's commitment and position on environment and health issues. • Promote use of recyclable packaging (aluminum cans, glass bottles). • Develop attachable "pop-tops" on cans. • Continue to promote alcohol moderation and traffic safety issues.

for the consumer" and recognizing that "everyone at Interbrew is a marketing person," for example, supported the need for respect and responsiveness. Each value was embodied by the *behaviors* themselves— the hundreds of actions that determined how Interbrew would act *if it were truly living according to its values.*

Management needed to make sure that people inside and outside understood who the company was, rather than just settling for further recognition of its beers, waters, and soft drinks brands, for it was the identity of the enterprise that fueled everything else. Making this happen meant finding a way to bring Interbrew's identity to life in all of its operations, from R&D and production to marketing, sales, customer service, finance, and human resources management.

The answer was to *reorganize* all the behaviors into six "change mechanisms," the basic systems used to manage the organization as a whole. These were performance evaluation, compensation, communications, training, development and education, and recruitment and employee recognition.

In each case, I created a detailed, custom-tailored "blueprint" to illustrate how that particular management system would operate if it were truly values-driven. For example, if performance evaluation were geared to putting the consumer first, then what would be "evaluated" would be employees' ability to make it easy for consumers to, say, get rapid responses to their questions or complaints (Exhibit Six).

Every change mechanism was developed within the context of all six values. With the help of Interbrew managers, I was devising a *values implementation* process that would become central to identity-based management. To engage employees directly and deeply was to get them not only to solve their own problem but also to create their own future. For Interbrew, values implementation made leadership by example the operating standard for all concerned.

A surprising thing usually happens in this process. Management's credibility with employees, and thus its influence, increases significantly. This is because company leaders can now say, "These ideas came from you; you told me to do this." Top executives gain immeasurable stature with the rank and file, for they have both listened and established a dialogue of substance that breeds mutual respect.

EXHIBIT SIX

Performance Evaluation

Performance evaluation is designed to set detailed performance criteria and, in doing so, to address all aspects of employees' jobs — the "hard," specific, day-to-day responsibilities, as well as the "soft," general cultural responsibilities which come with being a member of the Interbrew team.

Change Mechanism		
Values	Putting the *Consumer First*	A **Craftsman-like Dedication to** *Quality*

Philosophies and Supporting Actions (Examples)	*Make it easy on the consumer:*
	• Establish a centralized Consumer Response Center to 1) answer complaints immediately and 2) route consumer feedback to the appropriate group(s).
	
	Anticipate, don't react:
	• Never run out of stock at point of sale.
	
	Marketing is the bridge to the consumer:
	• Make a science of understanding occasions and purchase dynamics.
	• Make market research into the "consumer's voice" for the whole corporation.
		An obsessive attention to detail:
		• Set and enforce absolute product specifications acceptable to the consumer.
		
		Consistency is a measure of quality:
		• Special quality control for exports is a #1 priority.
		• Ensure consistency of packaging presentation (color, production runs, labels, messages).
		
		Quality is a personal responsibility:
		• Institute unannounced quality audits:
		  – Impact on budget allocations
		  – Executive compensation
		• Establish minimum quality control standards for cafe owners carrying Interbrew products.
		  – Correct beer temperature
		  – Clean glasses
		  – Clean environment (especially bathrooms)
		  – Knowledgeable/personable consumer-oriented staff
		  – Good location/good clientele
		  – Merchandising and promotion are current and well maintained
			• Institute a "policing" program through sales organization to monitor point-of-sale quality. Strict policy to "Clean up or shut down" below-par pubs.
			
			Making quality visible is a corporate priority:
			• Ensure all facilities are clean and well maintained
			  – Clean lobby at Leuven everyday
			  – All depots/warehouses/plants must have strict maintenance programs
			  – Damaged sites must be fixed quickly
			  – No dust on products
			  – Constant hosing down to reduce beer smell at breweries
			• Brewery tours must be "showcases" for Interbrew.
			• Refurbish delivery trucks/institute regular quality inspection schedule.
			  – Setting minimum quality standards
			  – Bi-weekly cleaning
			  – Replace worn canopies quickly
			  – Limit truck usage/constant rotation of new vehicles to reduce wear and tear
			• Conduct regular, surprise inspections to ensure (visual) standards are being met.
			• Establish quality standards for all corporate "media." Every form of communication must reinforce the quality orientation of Interbrew.

Continued

EXHIBIT SIX Continued

Values	The Constant Pursuit of Professionalism	A Passion for Communication
Philosophies and Supporting Actions	• Redesign entry foyer and customer lounge. – Exhibit Interbrew products proudly – Warm up lobby seating – Remove glass between receptionist and visitors – Eliminate plastic plants *Total Brand Quality:* • Promote the Brand Quality Assurance Program. *Quality changes with the times:* • Raise quality criteria every year. *The customer is #1:* • Every customer has a single "checkpoint" contact at Interbrew (for any needs)/ "Total Relationship Management." • Visit customers on a regular basis. • Let no more than one week pass without customer communication. • Every senior executive has a direct account relationship. • Establish a personal relationship with the customer. • Make regular point-of-sale site visits mandatory for international managers. • Respond to information requests immediately. *Everyone has a role:* • Rewrite job descriptions. – Focus on values, customer satisfaction • Have employees write/add to their own job descriptions at the start of each appraisal period. • Ask employees to write their own appraisals just before review time. • Provide clearly defined job descriptions, priorities, and objectives for every employee. *Your work is your bond:* • Be on time. *Raise your sights, set the example:* • Error-free documents; check 3 times; Spell names correctly. *Appearance counts:* • Establish basic dress standards. • Keep uniforms clean. *Take decisions, stay the course:* • Set and follow priorities (quarterly, monthly, and weekly). *Think profitably:* • Walk away from bad (Horeca) deals.	*Systematic communication breeds understanding and support:* • Establish monthly, time-managed meetings to review business unit performance and set objectives for next period. • Require quarterly strategic progress reports from top management to senior and middle managers.

Values	A Hunger for Innovation	An Unshakable Reliance on Teamwork
Philosophies and Supporting Actions (Examples)	*Knowledge is power:* • Look for, record, report trends, changes in the marketplace. *Risk fuels success:* • Criteria for marketing employees' evaluations include: – Revitalize old/slow products. – Launch 1–3 new products a year.	*One Interbrew, indivisible:* • New business initiatives are reviewed/signed off by multiple functions. *Missions drive teamwork:* • Establish targets (i.e., missions) for all teams (goals/impact). *Autonomy motivates:* • Teams set their own agenda.

The implementation began to take on its own momentum. As it did, I realized what was happening: As well as helping to operationalize identity, I was helping to *humanize strategy*—to make it accessible and meaningful to the thousands of people responsible for ensuring the success of this merger.

In the months that followed, Interbrew managers launched an extraordinary number of initiatives to transform the enterprise. The communications team devised messages to build support among a wide range of constituencies—twenty-three different audience segments in all. Each message was a call to action. Internally, for example, commercial (sales) employees were charged with being "quality control watchdogs and liaisons to consumers through the HORECA and food trade." Externally, Interbrew presented itself to retail customers as a "committed commercial partner," promising them consolidated billing and more coordinated deliveries.

A four-part employee involvement process was designed and implemented around Interbrew's thirst for life. It included a Great Performers recognition program, values education, training and development, and community activities that revolved around sports-related sponsorships, a "safe home" alcohol safety initiative, and funding for local environmental causes.

One of the most meaningful changes came about in Interbrew's performance management system. Job descriptions changed from cold, lifeless, third-person recitations of "accountabilities" to *personal commitment statements* focused on contribution and results. The description for the marketing manager for core market brands now described "my job" (as opposed to *the* job) as reaching specific market share and brand image goals in support of Interbrew's strategy. Another section linked this manager's success with how well he adhered to the company's identity-based values. The final part focused on customer satisfaction. Here, the manager brought the document to life by identifying his primary customers. He wrote down the names of particular individuals with whom he needed to build a relationship—and to whom he would be accountable in the course of the next year.

At the same time as we were reworking key job descriptions, we were also taking a fresh look at performance evaluation standards. In the end, these too changed. Among other things, the grading system was revised to foster higher performance standards in all functions, company-wide.

One of the main external initiatives revolved around inproving customer satisfaction. For several months, I worked with a special customer satisfaction team to translate Interbrew's identity and supporting values into a framework for strengthening customer relationships.

One of the first activities was to identify examples of employees and their "customers." These examples were then hard-wired into the performance appraisal process. Brand managers' customers included retail buyers, advertising agencies, and, of course, consumers. Truck drivers, the core of Interbrew's delivery system, were trained to focus on their relationships with café owners and supermarket managers. No longer would dirty trucks and unkempt uniforms be tolerated. Each driver "was Interbrew" and needed to reflect the organization's thirst for life and the pride that came with it. Receptionists and telephone operators also were included. Their charter was to view as customers, everyone from secretaries to vendors, and other visitors to Interbrew.

Many customer satisfaction initiatives were drawn directly from the hundreds of behaviors that had surfaced in the employee focus groups. For example, commercial managers (the sales force) were charged with the responsibility of working according to new service, quality control, and customer education and information standards. Technical employees (those in logistics and transportation) had to enforce higher standards in cleaning and maintaining all facilities and in their regular inspection and refurbishment schedules for delivery trucks.

Among the most effective tools the team developed were customer satisfaction worksheets, one for internal customers and one for external customers. Their effectiveness stemmed from the fact that employees essentially "designed" their own customer relationships. Each employee was asked to answer a series of simple questions: *What is the nature of the relationship between you and this stakeholder group (such as restaurant owners)? What do you do for them? (That is, how do you help them?) And what to they do for you? (That is, how do they help you?)* To ensure accountability, the worksheets were then distributed to particular customers identified by the employee.

For all the systemic change that was taking place at Interbrew, it was also important to effect *symbolic* change. People needed to be surrounded by visual reminders that Interbrew was unique, not simply the sum of the parts of Artois and Piedboeuf. Achieving this goal fell to the design team. During the two years I worked with Interbrew, the company went through an extensive graphic identification program. Everything changed: the company's logotype; its brewery and office signage, trucks, uniforms, stationery, and sales and marketing collateral; selected product packaging; recruiting, orientation, and training and development literature. Everything looked different—by design.

If design serves one purpose above all others, it is to signal change born of a company's true identity. It is to make it impossible for people, most notably employees, to "see themselves" as anything but part of that change. Design is an elemental tool of identity-based management.

Interbrew was *driven by a need to celebrate a thirst for life*—ten simple words that helped to make this merger work. By the end of the engagement, however, I had learned that no matter how perfectly they may have captured the identity of the enterprise, these words didn't tell the whole story. What makes identity unique to this organization, or any other, is how those words are lived, day after day, decade after decade.

~

A CALL TO ACTION

We are in greatest harmony with the Law of Comprehension when we are using all of our faculties to *experience* something: our sight, our hearing, all of our senses. In this regard, what we hear in the form of messages and what we see in the form of symbols are vitally important. The role of messages and design, however, is to shape expectations, not experience. From this standpoint, the call to action inherent in the Law of Comprehension is *"Show me."*

This seventh Law of Identity contains a paradox that explains why "Show me" is so important and also solves the mystery of *how*—how to effect permanent, meaningful change. It is a paradox that must be understood by all managers if they are going to succeed in effecting change and getting stakeholders to "recognize an organization for who it truly is." Call it *the transformation paradox*. As I learned with Interbrew, the transformation paradox works as follows. To make change stick, you need to make the "hard stuff" soft (business strategy must be understandable in lay terms) and the "soft stuff" hard (cultural values must be made concrete if the company is to thrive on the strength of its identity).

The Law of Comprehension demands that we take responsibility for letting others know who we are and what we stand for. The first challenge is to be comfortable and at peace with your own identity. Many individuals and companies are unsure of themselves; they lack confidence in who they are. *They may secretly believe they have much to give, but they are uncertain, and therefore unwilling, to take a chance on letting others know who they truly are.* To paraphrase the seventh Law of Identity, an individual or an organization is only as valuable as he, or she, or it is *perceived* to be. If you don't help others comprehend your true capacities, you are bound to miss out on opportunities that are rightfully yours.

The seventh Law of Identity is written in binary code: *Perceived* value is a black-or-white issue. There is no middle ground. This law demands that managers and the organizations they guide have the courage to step up and be counted. Anonymity doesn't pay. In the end, you will know that you are living according the Law of Comprehension when others, through their actions, utter two words: "*I see.*"

8 THE LAW OF THE CYCLE

**IDENTITY GOVERNS VALUE, WHICH PRODUCES
WEALTH, WHICH FUELS IDENTITY.**

*I am alive, I am unique, and I am immutable,
         even as I grow and evolve.
To truly live, however, I must express myself fully,
         and in this regard, have much to give.
But to do so, I need others, and am most productive
         with those who need me in return.
To establish these relationships, I must first be
         recognized for who I am,*
         and it follows then that
***I will receive in accordance with what
         I give.***

The circle has been invoked by many people as a form rich with meaning. We speak of the circle of life and the virtuous circle. We use the circle to describe the globe and, by extension, the knowledge we have, or want to have, about the nature of cultures, markets, and nations. Earlier, I referred to a "value circle" to describe the economic interdependence of stakeholders. But I believe the most interesting expression of a circle is in how it illustrates the eighth Law of Identity.

The things I believe I am—the "humanist/rabbi," the "strategist/architect"—prescribe my sense of self and foreshadow the gifts I have to give to my family, my friends, and my clients. What I get in return—the wealth I receive—depends on how adept I am at blending these two vitally connected roles. I do not expect to be "wealthy," as in immensely rich in monetary terms. It probably doesn't come with the territory. But I do expect to be compensated fairly in accordance with the contribution I make. Beyond this, I expect wealth in many other forms. This includes meeting people who are intellectually challenging, creative, and passionate about their lives and causes. It includes traveling to fascinating places such as Europe, Japan, Korea, and Australia. It includes the love and respect of my family and of others who understand the power of identity to shape life.

The loop isn't closed, however, until we understand that the wealth we receive in accordance with what we give fuels the expression of identity even more. For companies as well as individuals, wealth certainly is about money, but it is also about those things that, like a magnet, draw people back to us over and over again. For instance, the heart-felt recognition we receive from friends, from customers, from family members, and from employees "fuels" our determination to stay on course and redouble our efforts at whatever we did to win that recognition in the first place.

My work with then CEO Leonard Hadley and his team at Maytag Corporation, from 1992 through 1994, captures this reality. How Maytag Corporation lives, how its identity influences its business, provides a compelling example of the benefits that come with operating in accordance with the Law of the Cycle.

MAYTAG CORPORATION

Magic Chef Plant, Autumn 1992

The road to the plant was easy to miss. It was a sharp left off the main route out of the town of Cleveland, Tennessee. This was the home of Magic Chef, one of Maytag Corporation's recently acquired companies. I could still feel the warmth that blesses a southern fall. The leaves were still sturdy—a rich, dark green, with the slightest tinges of yellow. Change was in the air.

The plant was like many manufacturing sites I have visited over the years: a large brick and concrete structure whose edges were dotted with glassed-in offices and whose core was the productive heart of the operation. Manufacturing-based businesses often exhibit a familiar incongruity. Typically, the sites themselves are spare, no-nonsense, humble, esthetically forgettable places, yet they are at the center of the value creation process. They are no less than the "translators" of identity into the things that make identity tangible.

On that autumn day in Tennessee, I came face to face with a group of employees who were charged with telling me their views on being part of Maytag Corporation. The room we met in had medium-blue walls and a long table in the middle around which sat eight men and women waiting, it seemed, to be interrogated. I have always found a striking contrast between rank-and-file employees and senior managers, particularly those just below the top management level. Whereas the latter often are guarded, the former tend to say exactly what is on their minds. It is always an opportunity to learn.

Among those who participated in that meeting, one woman spoke most eloquently, in slow, measured tones. Her family had been part of Magic Chef for several generations. She, and now her colleagues, recited numerous stories about the organization; Magic Chef Company had its own lore that, over the years, had instilled great pride in its employees.

There was one thing that she and everyone else wanted to know. *What would happen to them if the Magic Chef name were changed to Maytag?* The question hung in the air like a giant Tennessee rain cloud, plump with precipitation, just waiting to explode. This woman wasn't asking what would happen to Magic Chef *products*, for it was a foregone conclusion that they would stay in the product line-up under their own brand name. She was trying to find out what would happen to the *identity* of Magic Chef, the institution, which had been in business for eighty-six years.

It was a question that went to the heart of the assignment: to clarify what it meant to be *Maytag Corporation*—not Maytag the brand, not Maytag the Company, but Maytag the parent organization. Inadvertently, this woman had put her finger on the issue of the day. In response to her question, I explained that the aim was to comprehend how all the operations that now were part of the enterprise added up to something larger and more powerful than any one could be on its own.

One of the hidden fears that finally emerged in that meeting was the fear that Magic Chef's quality, as good as it was, wouldn't be judged good enough to meet Maytag's legendary standards. It wasn't that these Magic Chef employees didn't think their products, or their manufacturing practices, were of sound quality. Rather, they were concerned that "the corporation" wouldn't see it that way. *The Corporation.* Every time the term was used by people in the course of our discussion, it seemed laden with suspicions and unknowns.

In response to these people's fears, I emphasized that my job was to try to help make this relationship work. I promised to take their concerns back to management. That was as much reassurance as I could offer for the moment. The issue of "the corporation"—what it really was and how Magic Chef fit in—couldn't be resolved that day.

I had done what I had come to do. I had identified problems that might stand in the way of making Magic Chef a productive part of the larger organization. The problems were all about fitting in. People were afraid of not measuring up, of not belonging. They feared that, ultimately, their relationship with "corporate" wouldn't work out and the company would be sold yet again.

As I drove out of the parking lot, I thought about the managers and employees I had met over the last two days and the many I hadn't met. Here "in the thick of Tennessee" was a manufacturing facility that was home to at least a thousand people who, like the leaves on the trees that surrounded the site, held forth against the onset of a winter yet to come. In their own way, they feared the cold—the cold that comes from not belonging, from not making the grade, and from not understanding why. What they didn't know was that Magic Chef had much to give to Maytag, the corporation, and not just in terms of production capacity.

Change Afoot

By the early 1980s, Maytag Company—the "dependability people"—had been in existence for nearly a century. In this time, the organization had established a crystal-clear reputation for high-quality laundry products, and not only among consumers but with employees and investors as well. Maytag was a well-understood, well-regarded enterprise that had become an American business icon.

The company's reputation came as much through its advertising as through its products. Since the mid-1960s, Maytag quality had been personified by *Ol' Lonely*, Maytag's lonely repairman who had "nothing to do" because the company's washers and dryers never broke down. Then, in the 1980s, Maytag appeared to be changing course.

Beginning with the purchase of Hardwick Stove Company in 1980 and of Jenn-Air in 1981, Maytag, under the leadership of Daniel Krumm, set out to grow through acquisition. The strategy gained momentum in 1986 when Maytag bought Magic Chef. The acquisition brought with it two other appliance concerns: Admiral and Norge. It also included Dixie-Narco, a leading vending company.

In 1988 Maytag acquired Chicago-Pacific Corporation. The particular target of that purchase was Hoover, a company whose heritage was as rich and storied as Maytag's itself. Maytag, *the parent corporation*, was now a portfolio of mostly white-goods brands with a leading floor care

operation. What it now meant to be Maytag—in terms of such defining features as product lines, price points, and even quality—was
becoming diffused.

According to Jan Cooper, my initial contact and then vice president
for corporate affairs, Maytag needed help in allaying the confusion that
beset the organization as a result of its acquisitions. The company had
"identity problems" that needed to be sorted out. In early meetings with
Jan, she described how confusion had permeated all aspects of business
life. Distinctions between Maytag Corporation, Maytag Company, and
Maytag brand were clouded. Managers and employees in other business
units were unsure about their roles and responsibilities.

Outsiders, including trade customers and Wall Street professionals,
simply weren't moved by what they saw as a relentlessly expanding
collection of appliance businesses. Among the analysts I spoke with,
there was a general perception that Maytag Corporation lacked a
shared purpose, or vision, to join the parts of the enterprise into what
one investment professional described as "an explainable whole."

To make matters worse, the company's two main rivals, General
Electric and Whirlpool, were gaining momentum. At the time of my
engagement, Whirlpool was seen as the pacesetter. Under the leadership of David Whitwam, Whirlpool's CEO, the company was taking
bold and decisive steps to globalize and was winning plaudits from the
financial community for its efforts.

The situation weighed heavily on the mind of Maytag's newly
appointed chief executive, Leonard Hadley. For Hadley, the role that
identity could play came down to several urgent challenges. One clear
challenge was to build Wall Street support.

Another challenge facing Hadley and his team was to strengthen
dealer support for the corporation's array of product lines and brands.
As satisfied as dealers were with the range and quality of the corporation's broader product line, there was growing discontent. Dealers
chafed over labored order entry, slow delivery time, and the large number of invoices they had to contend with in conducting business with
multiple companies—all under the Maytag Corporation umbrella.

At the same time, relationships with dealers were changing dramatically because they themselves were consolidating. As they did so,

each relationship Maytag had with a retailer, such as Tops or Circuit City, was that much more important. Not only was the number of dealers declining, but the *nature* of these relationships was also changing. Traditional "buy/sell" transactions were giving way to more interdependent service partnerships based on delivery response time, top management accessibility, interdependent training, and marketing support through advertising and promotion.

A third challenge was internal. Hadley described the pressing need to get employees to interact across divisions. At stake was everything from better new-product development and improved marketing to higher market share, *if only people would talk to each other.* A classic "we/they" situation had arisen. Maytag was discovering that it hadn't purchased simply a bunch of inanimate assets; it had acquired a variety of *living entities.* Each contained its own identity, and many of them, like Magic Chef and Hoover, had decades-old histories. It was no surprise that employees were holding fast to their respective heritages and ways of doing things.

Over lunch one day in the company cafeteria at Maytag's headquarters in Newton, Iowa, an employee captured the situation perfectly. She said, "There's always this unspoken suspicion about 'the other guy' when you don't know them." The fact that the employees of all of these Maytag companies were close cousins from the consumer's vantage point had never entered their minds.

As I listened to one manager after another talk about the ambiguous roles that divisions played, I began to see the toll confusion was taking on corporate productivity. Employees felt that every operation was being measured, as one employee put it, against "Maytag, Maytag, Maytag." News in the media about Maytag *Corporation* was often linked incorrectly to Maytag *Company.* Finally, and most important, I realized that the total value of the enterprise was being obscured by Maytag Company's dominance. Because of this operation's larger-than-life reputation, as well as its superior profitability at the time, the rest of the enterprise was getting lost in the shuffle.

Hadley had already made change a priority for the organization. In order to stay independent, Maytag needed to become more efficient and productive as *one enterprise.* Employees in many divisions now regarded change as "the only constant," but in a negative way. Some spoke reluctantly about "the new order of things" and about "change without purpose." One senior division executive lamented that everything seemed to be changing so fast.

A perception of Maytag as "a collection of pieces and parts" had taken hold internally and was even unwittingly reinforced in the annual report. Maytag's many acquisitions had led managers to present the organization as a *manufacturing conglomerate*. They had simply added up the total number of companies and manufacturing sites and offered them as a principal description of the enterprise. Here is how Maytag conveyed that perception:

- 1989 annual report: *Maytag Corporation . . . consists of 9 companies with primary emphasis in home appliances and vending equipment. The corporation has 26 manufacturing operations in eight countries and approximately 26,000 employees.*

- 1990 annual report: *Maytag Corporation . . . consists of 9 companies with 22 manufacturing operations in seven countries and approximately 22,000 employees.*

- 1991 annual report: *Maytag Corporation . . . consists of 12 companies with 22 manufacturing operations in seven countries and approximately 23,000 employees.*

I knew that this fragmented view of the corporation was missing the mark. There was far more to this collection of companies than these descriptions acknowledged.

The urgent need beneath all of these challenges was to define the unique role of the corporate being—to help it find its own identity and, as a result, its own way forward. The role of the corporation had become a hotly debated topic among managers, who held strong views about what the corporation should be and what it should do.

Numerous individuals saw the corporation's role as passive—an acquisition, financing, and coordinating vehicle in support of independent operations. The "holding company" analogy was used frequently. The corporation was a "service bureau" providing financial, legal, and human resources support. In many discussions, I observed the classic knee-jerk reaction that managers typically have toward parent organizations whose distinct, value-creating identities are unknown to them. They are the entities that these managers love to hate. They are seen as cash-draining, overhead-creating behemoths, and they are easy targets for criticism.

As much as this negative sentiment existed across Maytag's various operations, there were also a large number of managers and employees whose view of the corporation's potential role was more positive and dynamic. Many executives believed earnestly that the corporation could provide assertive leadership in terms of overall vision, centralized brand strategy, and business goal-setting. Among this group, the feeling was that "Len Hadley and his crew had to pull the place together as a symphony, not a bunch of brass bands."

Still others saw the corporation's role as facilitating knowledge and information through training and development and through enterprise councils. These "councils" would address such basic disciplines as purchasing, marketing, and research and development. Frequent positive allusions were made to General Electric. Never mind the competitive nature of the relationship between Maytag and GE; what people were seeing was the possibility of "the corporation" becoming the glue among seemingly disparate parts.

CLARIFYING THE MEANING OF "MAYTAG"

As much as I knew that I needed to evaluate each part of the enterprise on its own merits, I looked first to the heritage of quality that was Maytag Company's distinctive franchise. It was like the seductive tune of a snake charmer, calling me to it irresistibly. What did Maytag mean, if not quality? No analysis of the larger organization would be credible without examining quality as a pillar of identity.

The Roots of Quality

Maytag Company's history is as much about the quality of its ideas as about the quality of its washers and dryers.

The company was founded by Fred L. Maytag in 1893 as a small, regional maker of farm equipment. It operated out of an abandoned, thirty-by-forty-foot stove factory in Newton, Iowa. The farm equipment line was expanded to include hay presses and harvesting equipment. From 1907 until 1911, the company went so far as to produce "Maytag-Mason" automobiles in Waterloo, Iowa. The first clothes washer was built in 1907 as a sideline to the farm equipment line. Its purpose was twofold: to help fill seasonal slumps in the manufacture of farm equipment and to fill the growing need for a home washing machine. The Maytag "Pastime" washer was born.

Improvements to the quality of the Pastime came steadily. A pulley was added so that the machine could be operated by an outside power source. In 1911 a model with an electric motor was added. Four years later, Maytag created its Multi-Motor gasoline engine washer, which served rural homemakers with no access to electricity. In 1919 the company succeeded in casting the first aluminum washer tub, eliminating the chronic problems that plagued wooden tubs. It was known in the trade as "the washer that couldn't be built."

Expansion into a national company came in the early 1920s under the leadership of L.B. Maytag, a son of the founder. Under his direction, innovation continued. He conceived of a new washer design that used an agitator in the bottom of the tub. This was one of the most significant inventions in laundry appliance history. Its revolutionary principle was to force water through the clothes, rather than dragging them through the water with a "lid dolly." The product was introduced in 1922. Its enormous success put Maytag exclusively into the washer business and propelled the company to a position of dominance in the nascent laundry appliance industry. By 1927 the company had produced and shipped its first million "Gyrofoam" washers. Maytag's quality franchise was in the process of being firmly established.

The quality of ideas that fueled Maytag's growth continued with the first automatic washer, the AMP, in 1949. The production of clothes dryers was added in 1953. The world at large knows Maytag for the quality of its products, but its collective innovations was the genesis of the company's long-standing reputation.

~

For all its intrinsic worth and profitability, I soon saw that Maytag quality had a downside. With quality came a certain arrogance (*No one knows more about how to build quality products than we do*), and with arrogance came rigidity, leading to myopia. In the eyes of many Maytag managers, there was little room for the ways of others. And although most executives grudgingly acknowledged that lower-priced products could also offer good quality, it was a difficult notion for them to embrace.

As the minuses as well as the pluses of Maytag quality became clear, I realized that one of the major tasks that lay ahead of me was to affirm the importance of this most vital characteristic, while broadening how it was defined and practiced.

The Talents of the Enterprise

It was possible for division managers to "own," and thus control, their particular product lines, pricing strategies, and brands, but it was not so easy for them to control the *competencies* that had given rise to these things in the first place. These, I believed, belonged to the parent corporation. If I could clarify what these competencies were, I would begin to paint a picture of what it meant to be Maytag Corporation. The competencies would suggest the value-creating potential of the enterprise as a whole.

Standing back from the economic idiosyncrasies of each operation, I was able to sense far more similarity than dissimilarity in how they created value. With the exception of Dixie-Narco, weren't these companies all selling some form of appliance? Didn't all of these appliances fit into the durables, as opposed to the packaged goods, category? Didn't they often wind up on the floors and shelves of the same dealers and in the homes of the same consumers?

Each of these companies came equipped with its own colorful heritage and track record. Each, in its own way, had become an institution in the best sense of the word—an accepted part of the culture and society it belonged to. Knowing this, I reasoned that each had particular skills and knowledge on which their products, histories, and track records were based.

I evaluated seven different operations. Here's what I discovered about the distinctive capacities of each:

Admiral had specialized in refrigeration for decades. The particular skill of the company, however, was its engineering and design know-how, which could perhaps be translated into areas beyond refrigeration.

Dixie-Narco, despite being different in that it was a vending company, provided Maytag Corporation with expertise that served the larger interests of the enterprise. What this organization was particularly good at was environmentally friendly refrigeration systems.

Hoover had a history that was as long and rich as Maytag's. The company had become adept in two areas that were vital to corporate growth: product design and automation in technology and manufacturing.

Jenn-Air was the organization's leading maker of cook tops and ovens. In the course of achieving success in its field, Jenn-Air had become expert at product innovation and, like Hoover, at innovation in product design.

Magic Chef also was in the business of stoves and ovens, but at a lower price point than Jenn-Air. What Magic Chef was exceptionally good at was what I termed "customer (dealer) integration." Ironically, this skill had everything to do with price. I learned that Magic Chef had to fight harder for dealer floor space against competitors who offered retailers higher-end products and better margins. As a result, they had successfully refined their merchandising skills and learned how to work more closely with dealers who wanted to work with them.

Maycor was the corporation's principal consumer services operation. It served a variety of brands. What Maycor brought to the enterprise was not only service know-how but also an on-going feedback system for managers interested in tracking, from a service standpoint, the performance and reputation of their key brands.

Maytag was the quality center of excellence in terms of manufacturing. The other aptitude Maytag brought to the corporation was its passion and methods for training. This "training mindset" was a wholly transferable skill that other parts of the organization could benefit from.

On a piece of paper, I arrayed these various competencies around the name *Maytag Corporation,* without the names of the companies they characterized. Suddenly, the competitive strength of the enterprise as a whole began to come into focus. A picture of the corporation's inherent identity was beginning to emerge.

Management kept referring to the totality of their businesses as being "home appliances," "floor care," or "vending equipment." This view was far too narrow. Executives were looking at the business through manufacturing eyes and describing "stuff," rather than looking through the eyes of the consumer and describing *use.* This simple but important distinction helped to clarify further how the corporation created value. Maytag was "good at" five things that helped consumers live their lives: *cooking, dishwashing, floor care, laundry, and refrigeration.*

The true identity of the enterprise was going to be found in the sum of its operations. I had taken apart the pieces of this puzzle called Maytag and was now putting them back together to see what emerged. In my view, there was virtually no part of the corporation that didn't contribute to the value creation process. Various elements might play different roles and have different responsibilities, but this was *one* enterprise, and it needed to be understood as such.

In my time in Newton, I stayed in a local bed and breakfast called La Corsette. It was a small, intimate home that had been restored and was used often to accommodate Maytag visitors. It quickly became a place for me to rest and reflect. One morning I was sitting in the breakfast room with the owner, Kay, talking about what it had taken to transform the place into such a warm yet efficient place. Each bedroom was unique. The meals were of consistently high quality. The furniture was always clean. I commented to Kay that it must take a lot to make it all look so simple.

As we talked, I found myself thinking about the client, the people I had met, and the enormous potential I felt Maytag Corporation had in terms of its future. Maytag Company had been in existence for nearly a hundred years, Hoover for almost as long, Magic Chef for eighty-six years. Other operations also had long histories. Individually and collectively, they had grown, weathered various crises, made their way in the world, and established roots in the society of which they were a part. How could this enterprise *not* be alive in its own right? A moment later, I found what I was looking for. Maytag, the corporate being, was driven by a need *to improve the quality of home life.*

This wasn't just an appliance company, nor was it simply a manufacturing conglomerate. Maytag was a *home management enterprise*; this was the value-creating truth of the corporation. As I let this discovery sink in, other pieces of the organizational puzzle fell into place. I realized that Maytag's identity was defined by the collective capacities of the organization, rather than by its brands. The brands were the *result* of these capacities and constituted a bridge between the corporation and consumers. The role of each division, then, was to maximize the perceived value of those brands through their ongoing marketing and sales management efforts.

In a meeting with Len Hadley and his executive team, I explained that "improving the quality of home life" contained a call to action that demanded change in how "quality" was practiced. I needed to shake people out of their manufacturing quality rut. To help them expand their view, I proposed that they think in terms of *world quality*—a concept that would have little to do with geography.

World quality would mean several things. It suggested *a way of thinking and behaving* that encompassed everyone, including Maytag Company employees. It meant establishing *win–win partnerships with dealers*. World quality, I suggested, would demand *flexibility and an open attitude* on everyone's part. It implied a way of conducting business that entailed *a total marketing focus*, not in the narrow functional sense but in terms of how employees in every area approached their jobs.

World quality also meant celebrating *the individual profit potential and contribution of every division*, rather than just Maytag Company's profitability. Profit competition between divisions was strategically irrelevant at best; at worst, it diverted managers' energy away from creating value for consumers. Finally, world quality demanded that *training*, enterprise-wide, evolve from its largely sales-only curriculum to a broader, general management curriculum.

ON THE PATH TO VALUE CREATION

About two months after my initial presentation to management, implementation began in earnest. As it did, I pondered what actions would be needed to help the company capitalize on its new-found identity. One of the things that Maytag's passion for improving the quality of home life suggested to me was a deep, potential efficiency that had yet to surface in the organization.

How, I thought, could this efficiency be achieved? A key step would be to link all divisions in ways that enhanced their individual and collective ability to create value. In practical terms, this meant knitting these divisions together at strategically relevant points in their operations. From my prior experience with Interbrew, I knew that it would require, for instance, setting up competency councils. Such councils would focus on marketing and brand management, purchasing, information technology, and communications. To achieve the type of efficiency I envisioned, however—a strategic, or grand, efficiency—would require more.

In the spring of 1993, I helped facilitate the company's annual management off-site meeting. It was the starting point for making change happen. My agenda was to help Len Hadley and his team set a mission for Maytag Corporation. By now, my work had made the rounds inside the organization; the notion that Maytag was in the home management business wasn't news.

The session began smoothly enough, as I proposed the idea that the organization's identity provided the most logical "mission" for the enterprise. With the exception of one or two people, the managers in the room generally agreed. As we discussed the implications of Maytag's capacity for improving the quality of home life, one of the dissenting voices spoke up. With genuine concern and visible frustration, he made the point that the business of Maytag, in fact of all the divisions, was *appliances—making and selling some of the best appliances in the world*. It had been that way for decades. For him, improving the quality of home life just didn't mean a whole lot.

Others jumped in. The discussion took on a clamorous life of its own. As usually happens, two camps formed. In this case, one camp included managers who were comfortable with the mission statement I had proposed and defended it; the other camp rallied behind the executive who felt that the corporation's mission revolved around appliances. I stepped back and watched from the sidelines.

A few minutes later, after some of the tension in the room had been dissipated, I stepped forward to propose a solution: Why not combine the two thoughts into one mission? There was really nothing to debate; both statements were true. Maytag Corporation, as a whole, *did* strive to improve the quality of home life. And it did so by *designing, building, marketing, and servicing* what certainly were among the best appliances in the world.

The mission wasn't an either/or proposition. If there was a debate at all, it was the unspoken debate between *being* and *doing*. The identity of the enterprise reflected, above all, the organization's state of being—*who* it was, what it *stood for*, and what it was *capable of contributing to society*, one customer at a time. The fact that Maytag built and sold excellent appliances was equally important, but this was a *way* in which it expressed its identity.

The vital connection between being and doing was crucial to the mission of Maytag, as it is for all companies. To simply *be* someone or something unique and then do nothing concrete to express that uniqueness, is to abdicate responsibility for living. Alternatively, just to *do* things (to make more or better appliances, for example) could easily result in chaotic, inefficient activity. Being and doing were two sides of the same coin. It was my job to help operationalize identity on the strength of both.

One of the first implementation initiatives I led was translating identity into specific actions. Management needed to see quickly what it would mean to "improve the quality of home life." I turned to employees for the answers, using identity to unleash and channel their creativity.

We began the process by dividing Maytag's need to improve the quality of home life into three sequential categories. These categories included the consumer *benefits* implied by identity; how the company might *respond* in order to provide these benefits; and, what *actions*, or behaviors, were called for to bring about this response (Exhibit Seven).

Among many others, the *benefits* employees saw in improving the quality of home life included ease of use, more leisure time, greater simplicity in living, speed, and even greater pride in managing the home. How might Maytag *respond* to help consumers realize these benefits? Numerous ideas were proposed: twelve-hour (rather than twenty-four-hour) turnaround time on repairs and delivery of replacement parts; home tool kits and readily available, snap-on replacement parts for do-it-yourselfers; annual "home management audits" of all appliances, whether Maytag's or someone else's; and after-sale, telephone follow-up calls to consumers by line employees.

EXHIBIT SEVEN

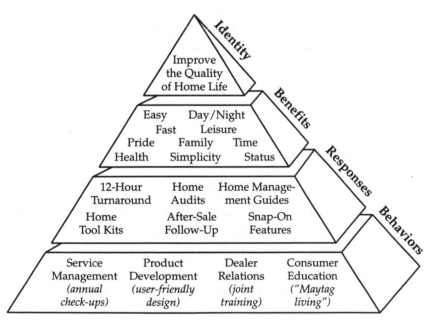

One employee proposed that Maytag author and distribute home management guides that would provide a variety of facts and information about cooking and food preparation, refrigeration, dishwashing, laundry, and floor care. It was a way, he argued, to deepen the company's relationships with people.

It was in translating these responses into practical *actions* that Maytag could begin to bring its identity to life. In line with the types of responses that had been identified, the managers who were working with me suggested several areas as primary targets for change: service management, product development, dealer relations, and consumer education.

At the same time as these systemic changes were being weighed, Len Hadley was leading the organization through a top-to-bottom corporate identification initiative. As with Interbrew, the need to surround people with visible symbols of change was of paramount importance. All stakeholders, particularly employees, needed to be constantly reminded that things weren't going to be the same anymore.

At its best, corporate identification provides the external signs of something deeper—the true identity of the enterprise. Its power lies in the simple fact that we are all intensely visual; sight is a central means of how we engage the world, whether it be within the context of business or of life in general. "I'll believe it when I see it" is a call to action for managers seeking to signal change and to differentiate organizations on the strength of who they actually are. In Maytag's case, the corporate identification initiative culminated in adopting the name Maytag for every division except Hoover and Dixie-Narco. The meaning of Maytag was truly going to change.

Gauging Results

The results of identity management initiatives must be measured. Some opportunities for quantification readily come to mind: *Customer* satisfaction and loyalty is one, *employee* satisfaction and commitment a second. Other means of quantifying results include tracking growth in sales and market share.

But the most important "result" of identity-based management is the overall productivity of an enterprise broadly defined—specifically, the *productive contribution* of employees to the lives of the customers and society they serve. It there is one financial metric that holds promise in this regard, it is a company's *return on payroll investment*—the ratio between payroll and such key measures as revenue, operating profit, the value of production output by location, and stock market capitalization. It is all about teamwork on a grand scale.

Still, the benefits of identity-based management aren't limited to direct economic results. To measure it exclusively on an economic basis diminishes the opportunity for gain. It is said that *everything that can be counted doesn't always count, and everything that counts can't always be counted*. Morale, passion, dedication, conviction, and invention are among these less easily quantifiable "things." Are they valuable to a business? Do they influence productivity? Absolutely. They are all the stuff of identity-based management.

In Maytag's case, there were hard as well as soft business results that helped meet the original challenges. An early outcome was Wall Street's willingness to rethink its perception of Maytag's acquisition strategy. The corporation's innate identity contained a message that began to resonate with investors: *Maytag isn't just an appliance-manufacturing conglomerate; it is a home management enterprise*. Communicating identity in these terms helped explain the underlying logic of the acquisitions.

A second outcome was the streamlining of the corporation's invoicing system, reducing the number of invoices to dealers from approximately six to two. Once the value-creating identity of the enterprise was clear, it made sense to executives to let Maytag Corporation help simplify, and thus strengthen, its relationships with dealers and distributors. It was a material step in responding to what trade customers already knew: *There was really only one Maytag*.

In terms of soft results, the idea of "owning the home" became a rallying cry for the organization. As I saw it, this was a statement of strategic intent that honored the identity of the organization. Finally, there was growing acceptance of the name Maytag internally. As one senior manager told me some time after the assignment had ended, employees across most of the divisions "were actually talking in terms of being Maytag employees."

The benefits of identity-based management are never completely predictable. In the end, Maytag Company's discomfort with service (dependable products shouldn't need service calls) was offset by Magic

Chef's talent for *using* the service call as an opportunity to build relationships. It was a skill that provided a model for dealer service and suggested much in terms of how Maytag Corporation might conduct itself in the world. Moreover, it was a skill that revealed the broader value, beyond the products that were made there, of the Magic Chef operation in Cleveland, Tennessee.

Maytag Corporation may not be the biggest player in its field or the most global. What Maytag has in abundance as an organization, however, is integrity; it is whole, complete, and confident in who it is. Through the lens of identity, it is this integrity that yields a strong reputation and steady, profitable growth over time. Maytag, the corporate being, knows itself.

At the same time, the enterprise has the potential to achieve greater efficiency—*grand efficiency*—as it marches forward. Maytag Corporation has every prospect of being around a hundred years from now. To be sure, the company will not look the same, and appliances will be dramatically different in the future. How value is created a hundred years from now is likely to be unrecognizable. But if Maytag is around, the organization's passion for improving the quality of home life will be there, humming away in the belly of the institution like a gyroscope, keeping things ordered and in balance.

Getting Paid

As much as identity-based management is about giving, it is also about receiving. This is a central message of the Law of the Cycle. Living according to identity is not an altruistic act. It demands wealth in return for value. No self-denial. No misguided sacrifice. How one defines wealth is a separate issue, but mutual respect is a tenet of the eighth Law of Identity. *One must be paid.*

The "wealth" Maytag receives in return for the value it creates comes in many forms. It comes in the form of unit sales, revenues, and operating profit. It is spelled out in consumer loyalty. It shows up in strategically advantaged trade relationships and is evident in shareholder investment. It can be seen in employee commitment and advocacy. In the end, it is all of these things that get "reinvested" in the organization, fueling Maytag's identity and its continuing march forward.

Throughout the events recounted here, Maytag Corporation exhibited many of the characteristics of the identity credo that explains the logic behind the Laws of Identity and contains its own rewards. Maytag, the institution, was indeed *alive,* a self-directing being with a mind of its own. It was *unique,* a fact best evidenced in the combined heritages of its operations and its distinctive quality franchise. Maytag was in fact *immutable,* even as it continued to grow and evolve. To change in light of its identity was for Maytag to become more of the home management enterprise it already was. Yet, how it expressed this capacity shifted relentlessly with time.

To truly live, however, Maytag needed to *express itself fully.* And so it did, in the form of growth through acquisitions that were largely in sync with its unstoppable drive to improve the quality of home life. In this same vein, the institution *had much to give.* To do so, to realize its value-creating potential, management took steps to liberate the ideas, experience, and know-how of its employees, all in the name of constructive change.

Maytag's productivity as an enterprise hinged on how it built *relationships with those people who needed it most* in terms of the value the organization created. This certainly meant its employees. It also meant giving more to consumers in the form of increasingly user-friendly products and service support.

Maytag has done a good job of getting *recognized* for who it is. In many ways, given its pedigree, the company had a head start. But it has a ways to go in terms of getting people to comprehend the true and fuller meaning of Maytag. Finally, I believe, the company has been *rewarded in accordance with the gifts it gives*—to customers and, through them, to society.

COMING FULL CIRCLE

For all managers, the Law of the Cycle can signal danger as well as opportunity. To focus on creating wealth before value is a recipe for failure, if not today, then tomorrow. Attempting to put profit before contribution violates this eighth Law of Identity and puts the organization on the road to self-destruction.

By contrast, the continuous cycle *from identity to value to wealth and back to identity* gives new meaning to the concept of the "life cycle" for business institutions (Exhibit Eight). Ironically, organizations are in some ways greater, more potent beings than the individuals who populate them, because their death is not a foregone conclusion. Organizations need not die, as long as their leaders understand their identities and take steps to keep the organizations' activities aligned with those identities.

Identity is both a beginning and an end. For people and organizations alike, it is the source of their unique capacity to contribute, of their potential, and of the opportunities that this potential holds. Identity is equally the beneficiary of its own strength: With exercise and expression, it grows ever richer, deeper, and more powerful.

Identity prescribes a closed system—in visual terms, a *complete circle*. For this reason, I come back to the circle as the most nearly perfect symbol of how identity organizes both business and life. The relevance of the circle to identity, and its special impact on leadership, lie in three things that are essential features of the circle itself—features that I first identified in connection with Alcoa and other organizations in 1987.

The first feature of the circle is its *efficiency* as a form, as in having drawn "a perfect circle." No other shape is as spare or as tightly prescribed. Similarly, the Law of the Cycle implies that there is an effi-

EXHIBIT EIGHT

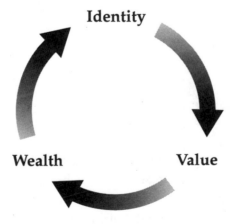

Identity

Value

Wealth

ciency to life—a grand efficiency—that is self-evident in its elegance and precision when all parts of that life are working in sync.

The second feature is *integrity*. Inherent in a circle is the idea of wholeness, or completeness. In this same vein, there is great integrity in a life lived according to the Law of the Cycle. The sense of completeness I have felt when I make decisions and take actions on the basis of what I know is in sync with my identity is a source of constant strength. I have witnessed this same sense of integrity in companies and their leaders, who, knowingly or not, rely on their innate identities as the centers of gravity for how they conduct themselves. Coca-Cola, Herman Miller, and Disney come to mind.

The third feature common to both the circle and the eighth Law of Identity is *endurance*. The circle—in particular, the circle of life—is the story of infinity. For people and organizations, the Law of the Cycle suggests a similar ability to endure. Perhaps human beings aren't in a position to benefit from this feature in the physical sense. But in the spiritual sense, we are. What we leave as a legacy and how we are remembered can produce value long after we are gone. The challenge of endurance that faces all organizations is enormous. Under the leadership of men and women who understand the Law of the Cycle, it is entirely possible for companies to endure forever.

The Law of the Cycle can presage great achievement and wealth if it is employed as a framework for organizing one's life or the life of a business institution. On the other hand, choosing to ignore it can foreshadow lives unfulfilled and wholesale corporate failure. Either way, the Law of the Cycle governs our fortunes, and the fortunes of business organizations, inescapably.

9 REALIZING THE PROMISE OF IDENTITY-BASED MANAGEMENT

WHAT WE HAVE LEARNED SO FAR

By its nature, identity isn't designed to be taken apart. In its form and application, identity is whole—the integrated result of one's unique mental, physical, and emotional capacities. Yet we have learned through this book that identity *can* be unbundled, at least momentarily, which is a good thing because we cannot benefit from what we cannot see. To peer into and examine the Laws of Identity one at a time—to understand them, experience them, test them, and apply them—is to demystify identity, making its enormous power comprehensible, accessible, and finally, perhaps, manageable.

In practical terms, what do the Laws of Identity mean for leaders today and people who aspire to lead? There are many steps that managers can take "tomorrow morning" to begin to align their organizations around their innate identities. Here, in summary form, are a few of the major implications of the Laws of Identity.

THE LAW OF BEING
Any organization composed of one or more human beings is alive in its own right, exhibiting distinct physical, mental, and emotional capacities that derive from, but transcend, the individuals who make up that organization over time.

194

The first Law of Identity reveals that organizations are literally alive: they are self-directing beings with minds of their own. Does this mean that they are self-governing? No. It does, however, potentially alter our understanding of the nature and practice of leadership.

The first implication is that *managers must serve the institution,* the corporate being, rather than the reverse. They must liberate its identity, bringing to bear all available resources to support it so that the institution's potential can be realized.

Second, managers must lead the organization according to an expanded definition of value creation that transcends profit. This broader view starts with the *human value* that is contained within identity—the thousands of people who make up the organization over time. Thus the life of the enterprise is a true reflection of employees' aggregate skills and expertise.

Managers must rethink the more traditional notion of *business value.* Under identity-based management, "business value" refers to the company's distinctive, or proprietary, contribution in the marketplace as measured by products or services that flow from and reinforce identity.

Leaders must also measure success in terms of how their organizations create *societal value*—for example, Alcoa's impact on transportation, energy, and food preservation. The deep roots that form when an organization brings about social improvement are an insurance policy of sorts; they set the stage for developing a long-term relationship with the marketplace that can help it weather many storms.

It is only in combining the effects of these three forms of value creation—human, business, and societal—that leaders can honestly assess the *economic value* of the organization in terms of its basic financial worth. In the end, those who serve as stewards of the corporation must guide it forward as the living being it is.

THE LAW OF INDIVIDUALITY

An organization's human capacities invariably fuse into a discernible identity that makes that organization unique.

The second Law of Identity asserts that every organization, like every person, is unique. What does this mean for leaders? It means that true and sustainable differentiation can be achieved. Moreover, if the enterprise is to thrive, its unique, value-creating characteristics *must be known.*

The imperative for leaders is to look deeply within the organization. *Commit to finding out.* Dig down; get to know the institution as the individual it is. Ask people—customers, suppliers, employees— what makes the company special? Ask them how they perceive your company creates value for them *and with them*—not in financial terms, but in terms of the contribution your organization makes to enhancing their welfare, their customers' welfare, the productive evolution of their enterprise, and the betterment of society. *Assume nothing.* Find the patterns. Peel back the layers of their responses and see what rests beyond such obvious answers as low cost, service, quality, speed and innovation.

Leaders who seek rock-solid answers must also look back. They must scrutinize the history of the enterprise for clues that reveal capabilities and passions that have always been there—and always will be. The seeds of Fidelity's *need to celebrate individualism* were sown decades ago. Knowing this made the discovery of the company's identity that much more credible.

When defining what business the organization is in, managers must remember that identity is the key without which this vital question can never be adequately answered.

THE LAW OF CONSTANCY

Identity is fixed, transcending time and place, while its manifestations are constantly changing.

The third Law of Identity speaks to the immutability of organizations even as they grow and evolve. For all managers who realize that life doesn't stand still and that their companies must change, this law demands a sharply counterintuitive response: "Change" initiatives, if they are going to work, must be wholly in concert with the identity of the institution.

Managers must come to see that the notion of change is already built into identity—into the identity of their organization as well as into their own. The challenge is to use outside forces—economic, competitive, technological, societal—as stimuli to spark new ways of *interpreting* identity, rather than as seeming reasons to change it. Korn/Ferry International met this challenge directly through such innovations as *FutureStep,* its on-line search initiative. The closer leaders get to aligning change initiatives with the true identity of the enterprise, the more naturally efficient the organization becomes and, thus, the greater their chances for successful transformation.

THE LAW OF WILL

Every organization is compelled by the need to create value in accordance with its identity.

The fourth Law of Identity describes a company's deep-seated need to create value on its own terms; *it must express itself fully.* Managers responsible for setting the direction of an enterprise must make it their business to know the identity of their organization in advance. They must either recognize the will of the institution as a central, value-creating force or be prepared to see their organization falter as, I believe, happened with Upjohn. Except by the wholesale disassembly of the organization, identity cannot be extinguished.

What is the upshot of this? It is a matter of priorities. *Identity precedes strategy.* If the direction of a company is to have staying power— call it vision, mission, purpose, or strategy—leaders must ensure that it flows from identity.

THE LAW OF POSSIBILITY

Identity foreshadows potential.

The fifth Law of Identity reveals the power of identity as a window on opportunity. What does this mean for leaders who want their organizations to grow? It means that the richest avenues with the greatest potential for growth lie in understanding the natural drive of the organization.

Managers who chase new markets solely because they are "high-growth" and managers who seek diversification simply to smooth the ups and downs of business cycles are focusing in the wrong places. They must first look at the value-creating potential inherent in the identity of their institutions if they want to grow in ways that are natural as well as profitable. Westinghouse failed to make this connection and helped to ensure its own demise.

Leaders need to keep in mind that their organization—the corporate being—strives to exercise and deepen its own identity; it seeks self-actualization. *This means growth.* Leaders must employ identity as a guide to growth while keeping economic requirements in mind. In view of identity, however, they must also rethink what constitute "reasonable" payback time horizons and "acceptable" rates of return.

THE LAW OF RELATIONSHIP

Organizations are inherently relational, and those relationships are only as strong as the natural alignment between the identities of the participants.

The sixth Law of Identity explains why organizations are *most productive with those who need them in return.* It is a case of interdependence on the highest order, yielding an entire framework for leading on the strength of relationships.

Leaders must recognize that a company's relationships with all of its constituencies must be managed as the *system* they are, rather than as a portfolio of independent relationships with stakeholders whose interests are diverse. This system, which I have described as the *value circle,* is fueled by the economic interdependence of employees, customers, and investors. Managers must organize how the company works in ways that build upon this natural interdependence. The goal? To put the value circle in motion, and get it turning. To build momentum. To create a relationship advantage that will stand the test of time.

The value circle has more to say about effective leadership: Managers who claim that shareholders are the most important constituency are missing the point. What matters—the only thing that matters—is *optimizing* relationships among employees who create value, customers who purchase value, and investors who finance value. Their fates are inextricably intertwined.

That organizations are most productive with those who need them in return suggests something else that no leader can afford to ignore: *Need is determined by identity.* New York State Electric & Gas is driven by *a need to shape energy environments.* This need governs the company's relationships with all stakeholders, implying value in many forms. Managers must understand how the identities of their institutions align with the identities of their stakeholders—all of them—if a relationship advantage is to be had.

A vital step in reaching this goal is for leaders to seed the Laws of Identity into the landscapes of their organizations. Open up public discussion of these laws. Call for all employees to consider how the laws might drive constructive change. Use them as a framework for fresh analysis of how the company builds relationships.

THE LAW OF COMPREHENSION

The individual capacities of the organization are only as valuable as the perceived value of the whole of that organization.

The seventh Law of Identity affirms the need for organizations to be *known for who they are* as a prerequisite to building potent relationships with others. The ramifications for leaders are many. Anonymity doesn't pay. Managers must ensure that their organization's unique capacity to create value is well understood. How else can people hope to make informed judgments about whether a relationship is worth pursuing?

Current and future employees must know the identity of the enterprise that they help form if they are going to live it, keeping it fresh, vital, and relevant. Investors also need to know the company's identity, for identity is a key driver of wealth. The challenge with customers is different; it is to make sure that they *experience* identity at every turn. Whether they can articulate a company's identity is far less important. What this suggests is the crucial role of employee involvement in making identity "known." If the leader has one job above all, it is to find every conceivable way to ensure that identity is hard-wired into the day-to-day operations of the enterprise.

What mattered most for Interbrew, the European beverage concern, were the details: increasing delivery truck drivers' authority to make filling decisions at hotels, restaurants and cafés en route, and retraining the sales force to communicate to retail customers what the company's need *to celebrate a thirst for life* meant for them in terms of flexible shelf stocking and return policies.

There is a corollary to this last point. Leaders must always keep *the transformation paradox* squarely in mind. They must take steps to make "the hard stuff (business strategy) soft" and the "soft stuff (identity) hard."

As a rule, employees cannot relate personally to business strategy and economic goals. Both are too rational and too abstract; they lack the emotional reference point that people need to make them their own. Further, most employees aren't in a position to have a direct impact on either. To be embraced by the organization, these things must be *humanized*—articulated through the lens of identity. At the same time, if they are to make a lasting difference in the growth and performance of the enterprise, managers must help to translate soft, though powerful, concepts into concrete behaviors.

THE LAW OF THE CYCLE
Identity governs value, which produces wealth, which fuels identity.

The eighth Law of Identity states that organizations *will receive in accordance with what they give.* What are the implications for leaders? The mandate is *not to put profit before contribution.* A leader who does so risks eroding the identity of the organization that is responsible for both.

There is more. If the intent is to "get rich"—to achieve wealth in all its forms—then, as was the case with Maytag, managers must marshal all the talents of the organization in the name of value creation. They must understand how the company makes a proprietary contribution and invest in these capacities constantly. Exactly what does this mean? It means that managers must challenge people to think, act, and measure their progress according to the cause-and-effect relationships that the eighth Law of Identity reveals: *Identity governs value, which produces wealth, which fuels identity.*

In charging their organizations to embrace the realities contained in the eighth Law of Identity, leaders can point to extraordinary benefits for all: *grand efficiency* that dramatically broadens the meaning and measures of productivity; *integrity* that reflects the power of the enterprise as one—that the whole is truly greater than the sum of its parts; and *endurance* that suggests the company's potential to live well beyond the moment and to deepen its intrinsic worth in the process. Leaders must work to achieve these benefits always.

In sum, what we have learned so far is that identity organizes life: the life of the leader, the life of the institution, the life that each of us lives every day. In so doing, identity answers vital questions: *Who are we? What do we stand for? What is our potential for creating value? And how do we realize that potential?* For organizations, the bottom line is this: Crack the code on identity, and you will understand how your company really makes money.

THE HUMAN IMPERATIVE

The Laws of Identity call upon our deepest capacities as managers, as professionals, and simply as human beings to understand and to "see" things more fully and clearly than ever before. What is visible is only the surface: the products and services a company is most often known by, and the things people say about them; the clothes we wear, the color of our skin, and the things people say about us. Beneath the surface is where we find the richest vein of gold.

In the name of understanding, managers need to take a fresh look at "the numbers" to see what they really represent. As organizations grow more sophisticated in the development and application of business metrics, they must find ways to measure their efforts at creating value. In other words, *metrics must be devised to test the success of identity-based management.*

Standard measures take on new and deeper meaning in view of identity. Does the company's image—the customer's view of the enterprise—reflect who it truly is and how it actually creates value? What revenue and profit gains are to be had if they do? What are the opportunity costs if they do not? To what extent are customer and employee satisfaction ratings traceable to identity? What are the implications for deepening customer relationships and for retaining valued employees?

Along with their ability to reenergize traditional metrics, managers will face the challenge of adopting new ones deliberately designed to test their organization's value-creating mettle. Measuring return on payroll investment, a concept I mentioned in Chapter Eight, is one such gauge. The ratio of annual payroll investment to operating profit, sales value, or market value is one metric that promises to bring into focus the intimate relationship between the creation of value and the creation of wealth.

To be successful as agents of change and growth, managers must recognize that identity's effects on leadership are both natural and cumulative.

- The first effect that identity has on leadership is *personal*. Identity shifts leadership from a position-centered activity (the CEO, the head of customer service, the scoutmaster, the captain of the football team) to a way of life wherein each of us is first accountable for "leading" ourselves forward on the strength of our unique abilities. Knowing where we fit best, and where we don't fit—which business, which profession, which company— is a natural outcome of living according to one's identity.

- The second effect is *organizational*. The presence of corporate identity (for instance, Maytag's need *to improve the quality of home life*) makes the institution's ability to lead, rather than the individual's, paramount. And everyone (more to the point, *everyone who fits*) plays a role in helping the institution "get there."

- The third effect that identity has on leadership is *managerial*. As a way of life, where the institution transcends the individual in importance, "leadership" becomes a comprehensive approach for managing a company, where the overarching aim is to realize its value-creating potential. From this perspective, a corporation's identity informs everything from strategy and organization to culture and operations.

Leadership is not about personal gain: making more money and getting recognition from others. Leadership isn't a reward. Leadership is an absolute obligation to live and grow through identity—your organization's and your own. To meet this challenge, managers must first lead themselves forward on the strength of their own unique characteristics as individuals; they must be recognized for who they are. Then they must promote among employees a vigorous understanding of the organization's identity, emphasizing that above all other assets, identity is the wellspring of value creation. Third, they must organize and operate the company in ways that liberate identity throughout it.

Humanizing the enterprise

The next logical step is for leaders to structure the organization in ways that fuse it with the minds, bodies, and hearts of the human beings it so passionately pursues: customers, employees, and investors. Why must this occur, and how can it be done?

Corporations were originally formed in part as a way to assemble, organize, and deploy labor and capital on a large scale. In many ways, companies were intended to do what people did: make and sell things. Like the machines at their core, these entities were designed in mechanistic ways that allowed for the greatest possible control. In simple terms, the plan was to minimize the human element in order to maximize efficiency. The organizations that people were busy creating, however, were *alive*—as alive as the people within them. But they didn't know it. To this day, we still do not fully comprehend what we have done.

As individuals, we do not operate ourselves as machines. It would never occur to us to do so. We are too multifaceted, too complex, too *human*. The only entity that can possibly be "built" from human beings is another living thing. Why, then, do leaders continue to structure organizations in ways that bear no relationship to how human beings function? Why do we routinely think and speak in terms of "divisions," "operations," and "units"—the pieces and parts of an enterprise—rather than acknowledging the totality of the being? It is simply because that is what we were taught; that's the way it has always been.

The purpose of human beings and organizations alike is to flourish and contribute to the best of their abilities. Both are rewarded on the strength of these contributions. From this standpoint, a reasonable conclusion might be that organizations should be structured to capitalize on their innate human capacities. If so, where do we find a model of that structure? We find it by looking in the mirror.

What this suggests is nothing less than the gradual reorganization of the enterprise into three interdependent systems that reflect how human beings function. These are listed as follows:

The Physical System. The disciplines that form the *body* of the organization; the skeletal structure, flesh, and blood that are its basic anatomy. These systems are the bedrock of endurance. Such disciplines might encompass finance (capital formation, investment and budgeting), manufacturing and operations, distribution and logistics, and key human resource functions, including, recruitment, hiring, retention and firing.

The Cognitive System. The disciplines that constitute the basic elements of the *mind* of the enterprise—its rational capacities—allowing it to reason and to discern opportunity and the vital need to adapt. Cognitive systems establish the organization's capacity to think. Among these disciplines are business, economic, and market analysis; research and development; market research; and key learning processes, including training, employee education, and (as it is now described) information or "knowledge management."

The Emotive System. The disciplines that make up the *heart* of the institution and that are the drivers of morale and attitude, passion and energy. These disciplines are the wellspring of motivation in both quantitative and qualitative terms. They encompass all forms of communication—marketing, employee, and corporate communication. They embrace customer service, employee recognition, and performance management, including compensation.

Why organize in terms of the human being? Because organizations *already are alive.* There is another reason, however, that is equally important. With its unique capacity to reason and feel, to imagine and invent, to solve problems and to build, *all at the same time,* the human being is by far the most efficient value-creating instrument in nature. By contrast, the machine model that has dominated business for so long was designed to be *repetitive* in its output, rather than original. By designing organizations in the image of machines, we have unwittingly obstructed rather than enhanced their natural efficiency. It is time to get it right—to design organizations in ways that unleash, rather than undermine, their human capacities. Organizing them in accordance with their similarity to the human being is a natural step in liberating the productive potential of the enterprise.

The purpose of forming and *managing through* physical, cognitive, and emotive systems is to look at, talk about, and engage organizations in a different, more unified way. Recognizing the existence of these three systems forces managers to think more holistically about the business—about how value is created, and wealth generated as a result. The overarching goal for leaders would be to achieve for all stakeholders the grand efficiency, integrity, and endurance that come with realizing the potential of corporate identity.

How would these systems be coordinated? How would their respective powers be integrated? The prime coordinating body would be an office of the chief executive, and its principal members would include the heads of all of the three areas: physical systems, cognitive systems, and emotive systems. A new management committee—the *identity management council*—could be formed from the senior executive ranks of these systems.

What also holds these systems together, blending them into one, is the identity of the organization itself. Figuratively speaking, that identity sits in the middle of the table at every executive session. It is the gyroscope that guides the debates and decisions that take place.

This model of the identity-based organization reinforces the crucial role of the chief executive as *the first steward of identity*, the keeper of what has the potential to be an eternal flame.

What we stand to learn from organizing around identity can be used to build knowledge networks that yield new insights into the enterprise itself. What are the truly critical relationships "among the parts"? How can the company create ever-stronger bonds with outside stakeholders that reflect their shared human capacities and needs? How can these bonds be most effectively managed to deepen the company's competitive advantage?

Designing and implementing these systems will require a geat deal of thought and time on the part of many creative, committed leaders at all levels of the company. But the business logic of doing so is compelling: True value can only be created through the integrated efforts of what is an exquisitely human system, and this can be brought about only through the leader's ability to maximize the company's potential as a living being in its own right.

MANAGING BY NEW CRITERIA

Along with the broad implications they hold, the Laws of Identity can be applied to all facets of day-to-day management, which, when practiced in the light of identity, will help ensure the creation of value and wealth over time.

For board directors, identity suggests selection criteria for chief executives, such as a potential CEO's capacity for servant leadership and insight into organizations, as well as the candidate's ability to keep a discerning eye on the external environment. Another such criterion is his or her demonstrated appreciation for the economic interdependence of employees, customers, and investors. Another is the leader's ability to refresh what exists rather than tear it down, and to articulate the strategic implications of identity to the financial community.

For CEOs, identity implies, in turn, criteria for board composition—selecting directors whose experience and "world views" are congruent with the unique, value-creating characteristics of the organization. It also supplies a frame of reference for picking business partners whose identities are in sync with those of their own organization's, for making acquisitions that strengthen rather than undermine identity, and for selecting executives who, in like-minded fashion, will strive constantly to liberate the value inherent in the institution's identity.

For chief financial officers and securities analysts, identity supplies an expanded framework for stock valuation. Which companies' balance sheets and income statements reflect an ongoing commitment to invest in and operate in accordance with identity?

For strategic planning executives, identity is the ultimate source of competitive differentiation and the center of gravity that offers up new avenues for sustainable growth. Because identity is naturally efficient, it suggests criteria for investment as well as disinvestment—in markets, businesses, companies, and alliances.

For marketing managers, identity provides criteria for market expansion. The central objective is to identify and invest only in those markets where the company believes it can make a proprietary contribution based on its identity. Product and service development also can be governed reliably by this criterion: Create and market only those offerings that are clear expressions of the organization's identity and whose purchase reinforces the natural bond between the identities of customers and the identity of the enterprise.

For line managers, corporate identity supplies a framework for planning and running the business. It clarifies the value-creating role of the unit. It is a compass for making strategically relevant operating decisions, for managing relationships with customers and suppliers, and for gauging the contribution the business is making to the corporation as a whole.

For human resources executives, identity yields vital criteria for recruitment, training and development, performance appraisal, compensation, and employee recognition. For instance, identity establishes talent profiles of people whose experience, skills, attitudes, values, and passions fit, deepen, and enrich it. Identity also establishes a framework for effective employee involvement. It clarifies people's roles and purpose within a single unifying context, calling upon their unique capacities to contribute to building and "selling" the societal as well as the economic value inherent in the company's identity.

For communications executives, identity *is* the message. It is the cornerstone of all communications, internal and external, now and forever. How it is interpreted may change, but "the message"—what the identity of the organization is and how it affects the company's relationships with all stakeholders—is inviolable.

THE REWARDS OF IDENTITY-BASED MANAGEMENT

Grand efficiency, integrity, and endurance are vital rewards that come from living according to the Laws of Identity. But they are not an end in themselves. Flowing from identity, these three qualities converge into a higher state of being marked by two deeply human forces: *power* and *grace.*

As a consequence of identity, power takes on unique traits. It is not transitory or fleeting. It is nearly timeless as a result of the often permanent changes that come from altering the patterns of life of individuals and other organizations. In this sense, the power that flows from identity is power for the *good*; it is constructive rather than destructive. It benefits all people who are part of its expression, because it is based on making a genuine and lasting contribution.

Grace, born of identity, has its own special meaning. It can be seen in an individual's or a company's ability to do something that is inordinately difficult with apparent ease. There is grace in the suppleness of the line, proportions, and movement of the corporate being when it has achieved a certain grand efficiency. There is also grace under pressure, which gives leaders the strength they need to endure trials and resist temptations (not to sell out to the highest bidder on a whim, for instance, or to take advantage of a monopoly position to continuously drive up prices while providing little additional value).

Grace, born of identity, is the state of being fully and effortlessly engaged in the world. Authenticity and coherence are its roots. In a state of grace—corporate or personal—creativity is not dissipated in conflict, nor is energy wasted. Confidence and serenity are its hallmarks.

One of the principal benefits of operating through the Laws of Identity is a state of corporate or personal health that produces wealth not otherwise attainable. The physical, cognitive, and emotive capacities that make one unique are operating in tandem and at full throttle. For organizations and individuals alike, such wealth can be gauged in several ways that transcend money alone. It shows up in agility and flexibility, in perception that is sharp-edged and alert, and in open, engaging sensibilities that can lead to fulfilling relationships with all stakeholders.

Companies and individuals operating in such a state of health are very likely to realize their potential through productivity, through creation, and through distinctive contributions to customers, to markets, to industries, to society, and (no less) to families and friends. What is the most predictable outcome from this achievement? *Relationships that are deeply rooted in trust.*

A key by-product of living or operating from a position of power and grace is that one has profound influence over the lives of others, enabling them to unleash *their* potential. Living according to these laws and the credo they form brings with it the opportunity to effect meaningful change: to leave a legacy. Why? Because it is in the nature of identity—an individual's or a corporation's—to make a difference.

For people and organizations who follow this path, there is an added benefit. It is the unshakable strength that comes from being authentic and true to one's self, rather than being fake or fabricated simply to please others. Such strength breeds a confidence that is born of being wholly comfortable with who you are—and who you are not. No guilt. No regrets. No second thoughts, whether they occur under scrutiny from friends, customers, or investors or in the shadow of night, at 3 A.M., alone with yourself.

The state of health that attends a life lived according to identity also promises longevity—being around long enough to accumulate the wealth that flows from the value one creates. For business institutions, this can be a life in perpetuity, where value and wealth expand forever.

CONCLUSION

We have taken many steps in our effort to address the extraordinary impact that human forces have on the fortunes of organizations. But the march is not over. The path we are on is leading us inexorably to the heart of the matter: *to recognizing identity as the invisible, immortal core that governs organizations just as it governs people.* What we do with this knowledge—how we respond to the Laws of Identity as individuals, professionals, and business leaders—is a challenge each of us must meet on our own terms.

Can the Laws of Identity be circumvented? Can leaders simply ignore these natural laws and go about their business as usual? Only at their peril. It is possible to turn a blind eye to the forces of markets and competition for a time. But these forces will always sort out the weak from the strong. In similar fashion, managers can choose to ignore the Laws of Identity. In the end, however, these laws will act to separate companies that understand true value creation from those that do not. The former will thrive; the latter will languish and die.

The only real prerequisite to engaging identity as life's center of gravity is believing deeply in the potential of people and organizations to create value for others and to realize wealth in return. This is the imperative of the true leader. For individuals and organizations fueled by this belief, the Laws of Identity are there as a guide.

Early in this book, I noted how much time and attention has been devoted to studying successful leaders in order to figure out how they do what they do. But one of the qualities of all leaders, whether individuals or business institutions, is that each is unique. It is often this very quality we admire most. Thus it is a mistake to study others with the intent of emulating them. Doing so is a self-limiting exercise. We cannot be someone other than who we are. Instead, study yourself, or your own enterprise, to understand what makes you, or it, unique. Invest in those traits, and leadership will follow.

ABOUT THE AUTHOR

Laurence D. Ackerman was born in New York City. He received a B.A. in English from Carnegie-Mellon University and an M.S. in communications from Boston University. He is a senior vice president of Siegel & Gale, an international consultancy specializing in business transformation through corporate brand management and interactive communications.

Larry began his consulting career with Yankelovich, Skelly & White before joining Anspach Grossman Portugal in 1981. He left to found Identica, along with two others, in 1985 where he developed much of his early theory on identity-based management. Returning to AGP in 1989 as a partner, Larry spent most of the next decade refining his ideas and applying them to a broad cross section of clients around the world. His industry experience is diverse, ranging from health care, manufacturing, and consumer products to financial and professional services and utilities.

Larry writes and speaks regularly on identity and culture and their impact on business performance. He lives in Weston, Connecticut, with his wife Janet and their son Max. The website for author is: www.identityisdestiny.com.

INDEX